B. K. Taylor, F.R.P.S.
178 Tamworth Road
Sutton Coldfield
B75 6DL
Tel: 021 308 0752

WATERBERG FLORA
Footpaths in and around the camp

Gamsberg

1989

Kambazembi Walking Route

Bergsig Wandelpad

Alte Mission

WATERBERG FLORA

Friedhof
Begraafplaas
Cemetery

Contents

	Page
INTRODUCTION	8

AT THE RASTHAUS
Boscia albitrunca 11
Terminalia prunioides 13
Acacia erioloba & *A. karroo* 17

MISSION WAY
Albizia anthelmintica 21
Acacia erubescens & *A. fleckii* 25
Acacia mellifera subsp. *detinens* & *A. ataxacantha* 28
Acacia hebeclada 33
Maerua schinzii 34
Maerua juncea 37
Acacia tortilis subsp. *heteracantha*
  (with *A. reficiens* & *A. luederitzii*) 41

FOREST WALK
Peltophorum africanum 46
Combretum apiculatum with other combretums 49

KAMBAZEMBI WALKING ROUTE
Ficus cordata 53
Obetia carruthersiana 57
Croton gratissimus & *Securinega virosa* 58
Lonchocarpus nelsii 63
Commiphora tenuipetiolata & *C. angolensis* 66
Acacia hereroensis 68
Dombeya rotundifolia 71
Osyris lanceolata 73
Ficus ilicina 77
Kirkia acuminata 79
Steganotaenia araliacea 81

MOUNTAIN VIEW WALKING ROUTE
Erythrina decora 84

FIG TREE WAY
Ficus sycomorus 90
Rhus lancea & *Rhus marlothii* 93
Ziziphus mucronata 97

ANT HILL WAY
- *Dichrostachys cinerea* subsp. *africana* 101
- *Combretum imberbe* 105
- *Euclea undulata* 107
- *Ximenia americana* var. *microphylla* & *X. caffra* 111

ALOE CIRCLE
- *Sansevieria pearsonii* 113
- *Aloe littoralis* & *Aloe zebrina* 117
- *Commiphora glandulosa* & *C. pyracanthoides* 119

- *Grewia* 123
- Mistletoe 127
- Ferns 129
- Lichens 132

Introduction

The purpose of this book is to make your stay at the Waterberg more enjoyable by introducing many of the interesting aspects of the flora around the camp.

With a total of over 480 flowering plants and 10 ferns recorded, the authors had to confine themselves to the plants that were prominent along the various walking routes (below the summit) for most of the year.

The paintings, done mainly in the winter of 1988, are arranged according to the route on which they were painted. Tree numbers, taken from the "National List of Indigenous Trees", are attached to the trees, therefore it will not be necessary to follow every path to see each species. The numbers appear in the text after the botanical name.

As the majority of these plants are found in other areas of southern Africa, they have many uses and common names. This book includes only local common names and uses recorded for this country.

Although the plains at the base of the mountain form part of the "Thornbush Savanna" vegetation type (Giess, 1971), the plateau is considered to be the south-western limit of the "Tree Savanna and Woodland" zone, the only woodland region of this country and therefore a particularly interesting and important area. The mountain slopes include elements of the flora of the plains zone and form a barrier between the two major vegetation types.

The Waterberg Park was originally farm land and is therefore considered a "restored" wilderness area. For this reason, most of the fountains have been tapped by man at some time or another and foreign vegetation which was introduced, must be continually removed.

Apart from the lush ferns at the fountains below the cliffs, a particularly interesting plant, *Drosera burkeana*, was once found here. It is an insectivorous or carnivorous plant, called sundew, honeydew or flycatcher and was collected in 1899 by Dinter at one of the Waterberg "Quellsumpf" (fountains). Further searches for it have proved fruitless. Unlike the famous pitcher plants of the Far East, this plant has tentacles or glandular hairs on the leaf that look like pins stuck into a cushion. Insects are attracted by their appearance, colour and scent and get trapped.

The information on lichen was written by Dr. D. Wessels, a

lichenologist of the University of the North, RSA. The notes on cultivation were kindly supplied by Mrs. E. Hilbert of the Department of Forestry Nursery in Grootfontein where many of these plants are available at very reasonable prices. Growth rates for the specimens have not been included as these vary considerably in a vast country like this.

Anyone interested in the wood of trees, should visit the Swakopmund Museum where cross-sections of many of these trees are on display.

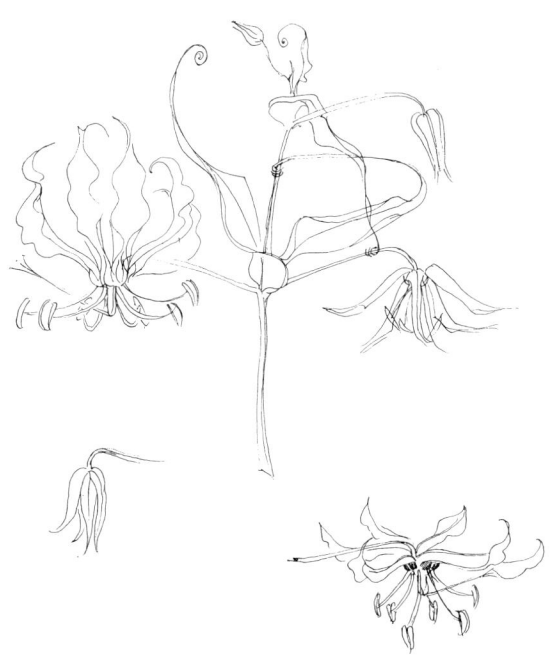

Gloriosa superba

AT THE RASTHAUS

Boscia albitrunca   122

Shepherd's tree; witgat (Afrikaans); Weisstamm, Witgatbaum (German); omungwindi, omutendereti, ozongwiṇḍi (fruit), omundjerere (Herero)

A French agriculturalist Prof. Louis Bosc, is honoured in the generic name of this tree, while one of its most characteristic features, the "white trunk" is noted in the specific name *albitrunca*.

When Burchell saw this tree for the first time and named it, the trunks appeared from "a little distance as if they had been whitewashed". This was near the Orange River where it was particularly common. The stem is often pitted with holes hence the name "witgat" (white hole). In some areas, including the Waterberg Park, the trunk may be almost black or brown.

Boscia albitrunca is found throughout Namibia and southern Africa except the western and eastern Cape Province. It also grows in Angola, Zambia, Zimbabwe and Mozambique. It varies considerably over its range and has distinct local forms, being either a small neat tree with a distinct browse line or a many-stemmed shrub. The leaves vary greatly in shape and size (from 2,5 to 5 cm long), but are usually stiff and leathery. Although this tree is considered an evergreen, its leaves may be lost at flowering time, in spring, when an abundance of small sweet-smelling flowers appear. The Herero believe that when these trees flower in profusion a good rainy season will follow and it is remarkable how in some years, the trees are yellow with flowers.

The green fruits turn orange-yellow when ripe and are about the size of a cherry. They have a rather acrid taste and slimy flesh, but are nevertheless readily eaten. Unfortunately the fruits do not last long, but can be made into a tasty jam or syrup. In the Kaokoveld berries, soaked in water, produce a sweet, non-alcoholic drink.

Boscia albitrunca plays an important role in the lives of people and animals especially in drier areas. Birds, monkeys and even elephants devour the fruit while the nourishing leaves are eaten by a variety of domestic and wild animals, including dik-dik, kudu and eland. The foliage is said to taint milk, but tests have shown that stalks and leaves have an

exceptionally high crude protein content as well as Vitamin A. The bark is eaten by elephants, as well as goats and horses in times of drought. Flowers are eagerly taken by antelope and hordes of insects are attracted by the scent. In some areas buds are pickled and said to be as good as European capers.

Research carried out by the CSIR's Division of Food Science and Technology has shown that the root of *Boscia albitrunca* could be used to preserve food. It prevents the growth of moulds. Local people have known this for a very long time, using pieces of root to preserve butterfat.

A coffee-like drink can be brewed from the fleshy parts of the roots, however it is not very tasty. When food is scarce in the Kaokoveld, roots are stamped and ground into a fine powder, mixed with grain, and made into porridge. It is also used to promote fermentation when brewing beer. In Botswana, the "witgat" has at times provided the Bushmen with much needed water, as water can collect in hollows of the trunk.

Although seeds germinate readily, "witgat" seedlings are difficult to transplant. Root and shoot cuttings however do grow. These trees are ideal for dry areas as they are hardy, drought-resistant and shady.

Boscia albitrunca is protected in Namibia.

Terminalia prunioides   550

Deurmekaarbos, bloedvrugboom (Afrikaans); Blutfruchtbaum (German); omuhama (Herero)

When without fruits, this untidy tree is entitled to no better common name than "deurmekaarbos" – a word meaning mixed up or jumbled. However when in fruit, *Terminalia prunioides* becomes one of the most beautiful sights of the veld.

Both the species name *prunioides*, Latin for "resembling a plum" and the common name "bloedvrugboom" (blood-fruit tree) refer to the rich colour of the winged fruit.

Terminalia prunioides is a very widespread species, common not only in the northern half of Namibia, but in the Transvaal, Botswana, Angola, Zambia, Zimbabwe, Mozambique and extending to Kenya and Tanzania. It adapts well to various habitats and is even found on the fringes of the Namib Desert.

In spite of being an erect tree along these paths, it is often a deciduous bushy shrub. Further north in Africa it reaches 15 m. The name *Terminalia* is from the Latin word *terminal* and refers to the leaves, which are clustered at the ends of short branches, i.e. they arise terminally. The leaves vary from 1,3 cm to 5 cm in length and usually appear before the small, whitish flowers which are arranged in dense spikes and have a far-reaching scent.

In the Kaokoveld young twigs are boiled in water to make tea, while the tree plays an important part in the ceremony at which young girls attain adult status. The Damara stamp and cook roots for use as a cough mixture, while in the Kaokoveld sap from chewed bark is swallowed for coughs, sore throats and stomach-aches.

In Owambo tree trunks are used for kraal fences and forked sticks support the main kraal entrance. Wood is used to make knobkerries and childrens' toy bows and arrows. Belts for boys pants are made from the bark. The wood is light, but strong and is used for tool handles. It is good fuel and makes excellent charcoal.

Terminalia prunioides

Fruits, leaves and shoots of the "omuhama" are eaten by domestic and wild animals including elephants, dik-dik and kudu. Giraffe also enjoy the flowers and elephant eat the bark. At times this tree exudes an edible gum, but this is not as good as that of *Terminalia sericea.*

The "deurmekaarbos" can be obtained at the Grootfontein nursery. Although the flowers are strong-smelling and rather unpleasant, they do not last long and a tree planted at a distance from the living area can give much pleasure from the long lasting brightly coloured fruits. It does well in warm dry areas in practically any soil type, including Windhoek although growth is slow initially.

Two other species of *Terminalia* occur at the Waterberg.

Terminalia brachystemma 548 is not common and seldom identified, while *Terminalia sericea* 551 is one of the common species of the plateau. Hybridization between these two plants can take place.

Terminalia sericea is locally called the "geelhout(boom)" meaning yellow wood tree, due to the colour of the wood, but the specific name *sericea* refers to the silky foliage. Apart from having edible gum, it has a number of uses. In Owambo the strong bark is used to tie the frames of houses together and grain-storage baskets may be made of it. In Kavango the bark of the roots is made into a sticky mixture to seal wato's (dugouts). On the Waterberg Plateau it is a very important part of the diet of eland and is utilized most of the year.

Acacia erioloba   168

Camel thorn; kameeldoring (Afrikaans); Kameldorn(baum) (German); omumbonde, orukarakaka (pod) (Herero)

It is not difficult to imagine why the magnificent trees that welcome visitors to the Waterberg Park booking office, feature in many of the traditional stories of this land. Although occurring over a wide range in southern Africa, Namibia's camel thorn trees are amongst the finest, providing shade, shelter, food and medicine.

Fortunately *Acacia erioloba* trees are protected today as they were used so extensively in the past that few large trees remain, especially in farming areas. They provide good fencing posts, spiny enclosures for protecting stock at night and excellent fuel. Wood was used for mine props, mohango pounding blocks, house building, tools and weapons. In Owambo, knobkerries were made out of the heart-wood of larger stems, while large poles were used for kraal entrances in the belief that they would drive away stinging bees.

The edible gum that hardens on drying is chewed from the stems of the camel thorn in Owambo, while in other areas the gum is said to be only eaten when fresh because of its sharp

taste and used medicinally for stomach upsets. Other uses recorded from Owambo include using heated pods to reduce swellings on the body, while wood ashes help heal leg, arm or foot injuries. In the past when women wore skin skirts, an oil obtained from crushed seeds was mixed with red ochre and smeared on the body as a cosmetic.

The Nama make a hot drink from the seeds and, when reeds are not available, flutes are made from the root cortex. In Kaokoveld and the Kavango roots are used as a cough remedy and the bark as fuel for baking clay pots. Pods were used for tanning in the early days of Namibia.

The number of animals that utilize various parts of *Acacia erioloba* are enumerable. The flowers which appear in spring are devoured by sheep and game, as are the leaves, twigs, pods and seedlings. Although ripe pods are said to be nutritious, green ones may cause poisoning. They are also probably responsible for milk tasting bitter.

Acacia erioloba is available at the Grootfontein nursery and grows well, if a little slowly. To overcome this, a fast growing species could be planted next to it, thus providing for the long and short-term. A suitable tree would be *Acacia karroo*, one of the fastest growing indigenous trees and common at the Waterberg.

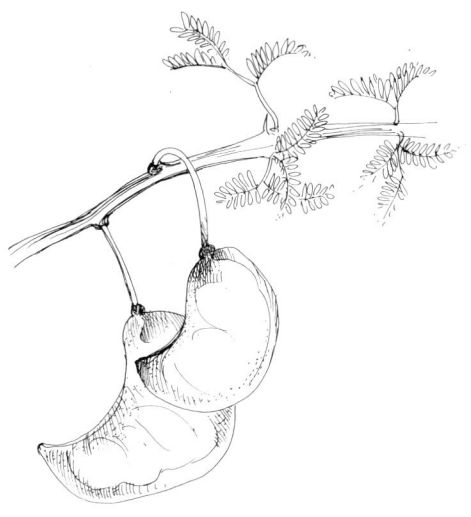

Acacia karroo 172

Sweet thorn, soetdoring (Afrikaans); Weissdorn(akazie) (German); orusu (Herero)

Like *Acacia erioloba*, the sweet thorn has long white thorns and has played an important role in the environment. It is the most widespread acacia species in southern Africa and its nutritious and plentiful gum is considered a treat by many children. This gum also has excellent adhesive properties and was previously exported from the Cape for use in confectionery. It was also used for book-binding and office glue in Malawi and for floor-making in Namaqualand. Baboons are often found in the vicinity of these trees as they collect the gum as well as insects and larvae on the bark.

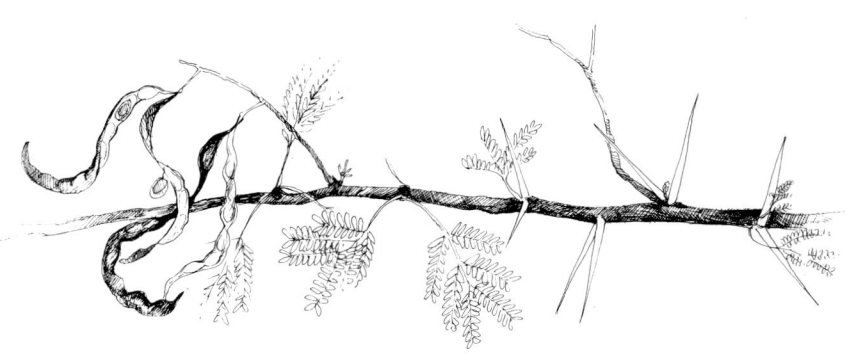

MISSION WAY

Albizia anthelmintica   150

Aruboom, oumahout, kersieblomboom (Afrikaans); Wurmrindenbaum, Kirschblütenbaum (German); omuama, omupopo, omuryandjima — food (okurya) of the baboon (ondjima) (Herero)

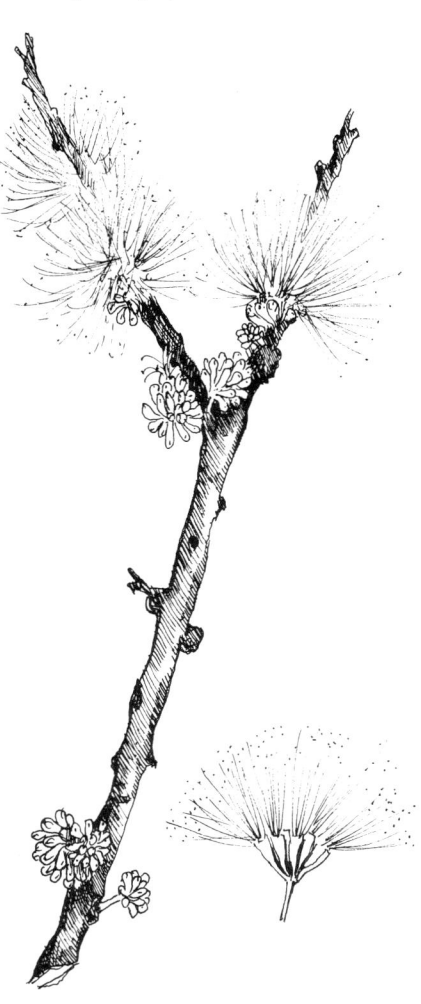

Although the flowers of *Albizia anthelmintica* do not resemble those of the cherry tree, the sight (and perhaps the scent) of the flowering trees in spring, reminded early European travellers in this country of blossom-time back home and they called it the "Kirschblütenbaum" (cherry flower) tree.

In this part of the Waterberg Park, the bark of many "omuama" trees is marked i.e. scratched, chewed or gnawed. This is no doubt the work of baboons who, like the people and animals of Africa, know the valuable anti-helminthic (anti-worm) properties of the bark (or root) of this tree. This is also reflected in many common names and the specific name — *anthelmintica.*

The botanical name *Albizia* comes from an Italian nobleman who over 200 years ago was the first to introduce a tree species of this genus into Tuscany from Constantinople.

Albizia anthelmintica is very widely distributed. It grows from Mozambique, Swaziland, the RSA, Botswana and Angola, northwards to the Sudan and Ethiopia, where the trees are noticeably larger. It grows throughout Namibia, except in the true Namib and the extreme south.

The "omuama" loses its leaves in winter, but not before they turn shades of yellow and gold, making the tree distinctive in the veld. These leaves and the pods, which are 12 cm long, are very like an *Acacia* species, however this tree does not have thorns. Sometimes young branches are spine-tipped.

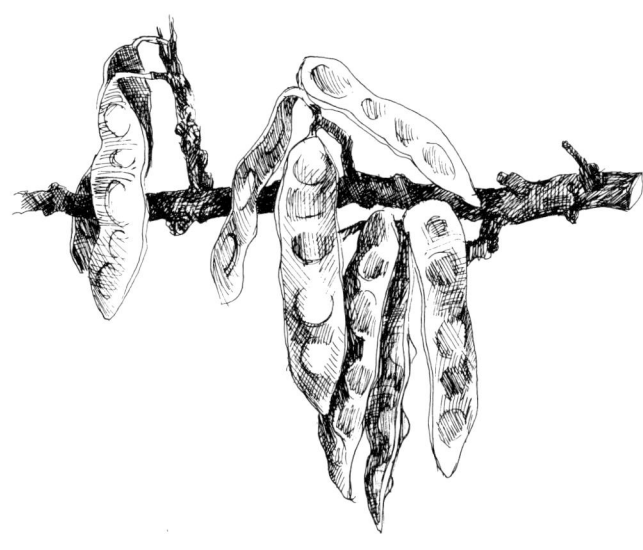

The bark varies from dark grey to a reddish-brown and is fairly smooth. Elephants are said to strip the bark in Etosha, but it is not only wild animals that are aware of its value — even cattle eat bark when infested with worms. In Owambo, where one of the local names means "to-drive-out", an anti-helminthic tea is made from pounded roots and taken for intestinal worms and stomach ailments.

The bark of *Albizia anthelmintica* is used by the Herero to thicken milk and the wood for carving articles like spoons, pots and basins. Small branches are used in Owambo as toothbrushes, the frayed ends serving as bristles. As elsewhere in Africa, Herero women take a decoction for contraception and both bark and roots are used in the treatment of venereal diseases, nervous and stomach complaints and as a purgative.

The "omuama" is considered good fodder. Small stock feed on the pods, while leaves and shoots are eaten by antelope. Pollen is said to irritate the eyes, especially of sheep.

Albizia anthelmintica is a protected tree in Namibia. Seedlings are available at the Grootfontein nursery.

Acacia erubescens   164

Yellow bark acacia; withaak, berkebasakasia, (Afrikaans); Birkenrindenakazie (German); omungongomwi (Herero)

Acacia fleckii   165

Sandveld acacia; sandveldakasia, blaardoring, (Afrikaans); Sandveldakazie, (German); omutaurambuku, otjitaurambuku (Herero)

Two of the most difficult acacias to tell apart, particularly in the dry season are *Acacia erubescens* and *Acacia fleckii*. The main botanical differences are based on leaf features i.e. the size and position of glands found on the leaves, the length of the leaf stalk and the number and the size of the leaflets. As *Acacia erubescens* is deciduous and *Acacia fleckii* semi-deciduous, accurate identification is difficult unless one is well acquainted with the trees in their environment.

Other identification aids are the colour and timing of the flowers as well as the colour of the bark and young thorns. Both species have pale flaky bark, both have small hooked thorns in pairs, however there may be a "tail" marking (about 13 mm long) down the stem below the thorns of *Acacia fleckii*. Flowers generally appear before the leaves on *Acacia erubescens*, while *Acacia fleckii* is in leaf. The spikes of the former are shorter i.e. 4 cm long, while those of *Acacia fleckii* may be 8,5 to 10 cm long. Both have pods about 10 cm long of a fawn or biscuit colour.

The German name "Birkenrindenakazie" for *Acacia erubescens* comes from the yellowy-white bark which can be removed in thin strips much like birch trees. The origin of the name *erubescens* (meaning "blush red") is not clear and may allude to the leaflets (as young ones sometimes have reddish edges) or to the flowers that often have a pinkish tinge.

It grows in the northern half of Namibia, in Botswana and the Transvaal and extends to tropical Africa. At the Waterberg it forms little woods of single-stemmed trees that branch low down, but can also be a many-branched shrub or short bushy tree.

Acacia erubescens produces a sweet-tasting gum that is reasonably tasty and sought after by children. The strong bark

is used as string in Owambo, while in the Kaokoveld it promotes curdling in milk. Leaves, flowers and pods are eaten by game and seed pods by small stock. Branches are used for making huts and kraal fences. The hard wood makes good fuel and has also been used for walking- and carrying-sticks in the Kaokoveld.

Acacia fleckii is named after Dr. E. Fleck, geologist and plant collector in Namibia in the last century. It is a tree that prefers growing on sand if its common name is to be relied on. In Owambo it is known as "one-that-ties-up elephants".

Acacia fleckii is found from here to Angola, Zimbabwe and Zambia, but also in Botswana and the Transvaal. It is usually a shrub, but can grow into a spreading tree, as seen along the Kambazembi Walking Route. Its gum is edible and the leaves and pods are eaten by small stock. Rhino and elephant eat the branches and various antelope eat the flowers, leaves and pods. Branches are used for fencing material and as gates for animal enclosures.

Acacia mellifera subsp. detinens   176

Swarthaak, nooibos (Afrikaans); Hakendornakazie (German); omusaona (Herero)

Maligned in Namibia, because of its tendency to form dense impenetrable thickets, *Acacia mellifera* is named for its one very pleasant feature – the honey-scented flowers, while its ability to detain by its recurved thorns, is reflected in the sub-species name *detinens.* This acacia is said to have more thorns per unit length than any other species. Another subspecies, *mellifera*, from the more northern parts of Africa, only reaches the Kaokoveld of Namibia.

Acacia mellifera subsp. *detinens* grows from the Kunene River in the north to the Orange River in the south, but not in the extreme eastern or western parts of this country. It also occurs in Botswana, the Transvaal, OFS and the Cape and extends northwards to tropical Africa. Communities of "swarthaak" are common on the foothills of the Waterberg, but they are not abundant along these paths. Some erect trees, 4 or 5 m tall grow along the Kambazembi Walking Route, and lower shrubs occur between the Mission and the Cemetery.

The leaves have larger, but fewer leaflets than any other acacia found here and they generally appear after flowering time i.e. spring, however flowers sometimes follow rainfall. The flat papery pods are usually very numerous and obvious,

changing from green to biscuit in colour. As the seeds ripen rapidly germination may even occur in fallen pods if rain should fall at this period.

Acacia mellifera is a pioneer plant that covers disturbed ground very quickly and is a serious threat to grazing. Much research is being done on the problem, but no answers are yet available. One report from the University of Stellenbosch, welcomed by farmers, mentions a "homa" fungus that is destroying this intrusive bush. The problem now is – what will replace the dead "swarthaak"? Will the invasive sekelbos *(Dichrostachys cinerea)* take over?

Acacia mellifera does have some uses. Besides the flowers that are attractive to bees and eaten by giraffe and antelope, it has edible gum which can be stored for long periods as it does not become sour. Leaves, pods and twigs are eaten by cattle and game, and in the last drought "swarthaak" came to the aid of farmers as young shrubs were ground by hammermills for feed. Although sheep farmers resent the sharp prickles, thorny branches make excellent fences for protecting stock. Stems have also been used for pick and axe handles. Wood is tough and fine-grained and makes good fuel. Debarked pieces of root are regarded as the best souring agent in the Kaokoveld and are used in calabashes of milk to promote curdling. In this region parts of the plant are also used for snake bite, while the Damara used a decoction of the bark as a cough mixture. Sap from *Acacia mellifera*, obtained by heating a branch or chewing the inner bark, mixed with the chrysalis of a grub, *Diamphidia simplex*, makes a strong poison for arrow tips.

Acacia ataxacantha 160

Flame thorn; roosdoring, rankroos (Afrikaans); Rosendornakazie (German); oruweyo (Herero)

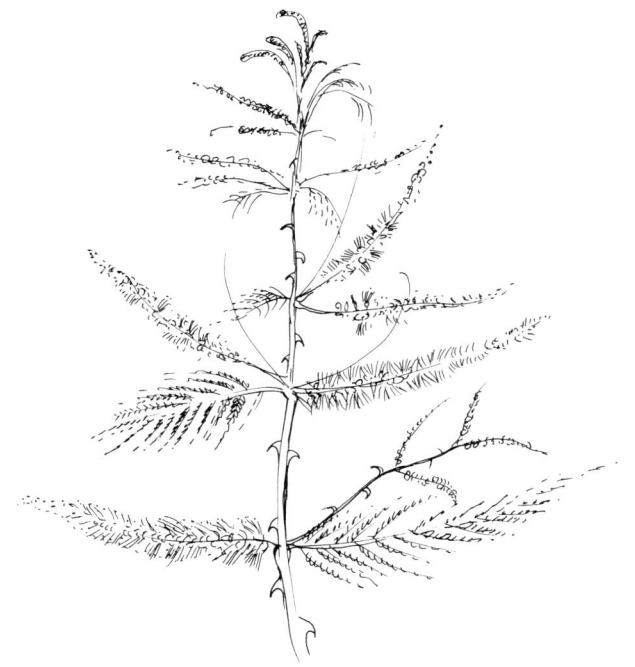

Like *Acacia mellifera*, the flame thorn has a tendency to form impenetrable tangles (up to 5 m in diameter) and at the Waterberg it is encroaching with "sekelbos" *(Dichrostachys cinerea)* on disturbed areas. It is not common along the paths, but the attractive scented flowers in long yellowish-white spikes and the developing pods, which are bright wine-red, make it conspicuous where it does occur.

Acacia ataxacantha grows only in the northern parts of Namibia, the RSA and Botswana. Like the "swarthaak", it has recurved thorns, but these are irregularly arranged. The leaves vary considerably, but have small hooked thorns on the undersides of the midrib and are about 13 cm long. The strong, but springy wood is favoured for making bows in Kaokoveld and Owambo and is used for roof supports.

Acacia hebeclada   170

Candle pod acacia; kersdoringboom, trassiebos; (Afrikaans); Kerzenakazie, Stehschote (German); otjimbuku, (Herero)

Due to the fact that *Acacia hebeclada* is very widespread and has many diverse forms, it has numerous local names and has been divided into different subspecies. The most typical and wide ranging one, subsp. *hebeclada*, is found here. The botanical name comes form the Greek *hebe* for "pubescent" and *klados* a "branch" and refers to the hairy branches. The erect pods that persist on the tree for many months and make identification of this species fairly simple are responsible for the name 'candle thorn' while another characteristic – its very hard wood is referred to in an Owambo name meaning "cut-by-fools".

Acacia hebeclada subsp. *hebeclada* grows from the north of this country to the south, but seldom in the dry west. It also occurs in Botswana, the Transvaal, OFS and northern Cape. It can be a single stemmed tree, but is often a dense tangled bush with a characteristic flattened growth form, as can be seen near the cemetery. In some areas, noticeably on the plains below the Waterberg, it forms thickets a few square metres in size, because underground stolons give rise to young shoots above the ground. In the Kalahari these thickets are frequently utilized by large carnivores for shelter during the heat of the day.

The "trassiebos" has paired thorns that can be straight or slightly recurved. The pale yellowy flowers turn deep yellow on ageing and when these heads are common (usually springtime), they make an attractive show. The upright pods are hard, strong and slightly furry. They dry to buff or a yellowish colour, but after a few seasons on the tree turn black. The seeds rattle when shaken and are used as anklets by some African tribes in their ritual dances.

Acacia hebeclada produces an edible gum and it may be one of the host plants of desert truffles that grow under the ground and are relished by people. Seed pods are eaten by small stock and leaves by cattle and goats, however at times during the year, the foliage may be toxic. Branches and leaves are also eaten by game. Wood is used for hoe and axe handles and fencing. In the Kaokoveld an extract of root bark is used to treat stomach complaints.

Maerua schinzii 136

Kwarda, lammerdrol (Afrikaans); Südwester Lorbeerbaum (German); etungu, omuhaseviwa (Herero)

In the late 19th century, Hans Schinz, a professor of Botany in Zürich, visited our country and this tree, which occurs practically throughout this country, was named after him. It also grows in drier areas of Angola, Botswana and to a limited extent in northern Namaqualand.

Maerua schinzii is, as a rule, an erect tree with a neat crown, but it may branch low down. The trunk is smooth and can be white or almost black. Trees growing in the desert often have interesting bent or twisted trunks. Leaf size varies from 2 to 6 cm long and 1 to 3,5 cm wide. Apart from having no petals at all, the flowers resemble those of *Maerua juncea.* The numerous (30-70) yellowish stamens, each about 1,5 cm long, make a lovely show.

The fruit also contrasts with that of *Maerua juncea*, being dry and pod-like. It is 13 cm long and the constrictions between the seeds make it look rather like a string of beads. They are not edible, but crushed seeds mixed with water make a palatable drink.

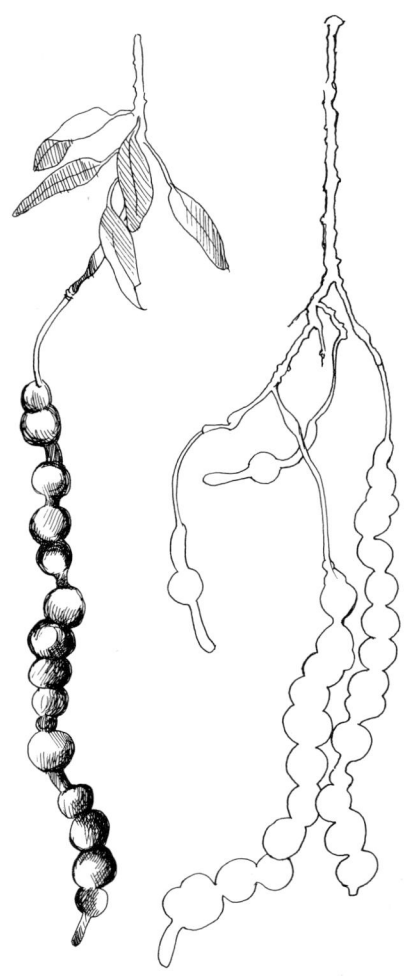

In days gone by in Owambo, *Maerua schinzii* was placed over the entrance of a kraal to keep out evil spirits. Stamped leaves were also inhaled as a remedy for headaches. The Heikum Bushmen used the root for heart ailments, either powdered and taken orally, or worn as an amulet on the chest and in Botswana other medicinal uses have been recorded for it.

Leaves and twigs are browsed by large and small stock and it is a useful shade tree. Unfortunately seedlings are not often available at the Grootfontein nursery as seeds are seldom viable. Seedlings grow extremely slowly and do not establish easily. Trees growing in their natural habitat are protected in Namibia. In some areas it is called the "kringboom" (ring tree) because the wood is said to dry into concentric rings.

Maerua juncea

Slangeierbos (Afrikaans);
Schlangeneierbusch (German);
omupangambura (to doctor the rain), orueti, oroti (Herero)

When the Waterberg flora is lush and green, this plant is not conspicuous. However when most of the vegetation is grey and drab (early spring), *Maerua juncea* stands out as a green mass. It is often perched on the tops of other plants as its straggling stem needs to support itself on trees and shrubs. The botanical name *juncea*, meaning "like a rush", refers to the appearance of the stem when it is leafless. The derivation of the word *Maerua* is from the Arabic "Meru", a mountain of great height.

Maerua juncea grows in Namibia, Botswana, Zimbabwe, Malawi, Mozambique, Tanzania and the Congo. The flowers have whitish petals that are only a few millimeters long, therefore it is the stamens that are responsible for the attractive and obvious show. They are very numerous and may be 2 cm long. Unripe fruits are green and rough, but become yellowish and smooth when ripe. They are about 4,5 cm long and 2,5 cm in diameter with 10 to 20 seeds embedded in pulp.

Mention is seldom made in reports of *Maerua juncea* of edible fruit and only the following uses have been recorded. It is readily eaten by stock. The Damara consider it a life-saving plant, because a root decoction which causes vomiting is given in the event of poisoning. In Owambo, crushed twigs are put into water troughs to protect cattle from anthrax, while its Herero name is derived from reputed supernatural powers with regard to rain i.e. the stems can be burnt to stop the rain during floods.

In areas where *Maerua juncea* occurs naturally, it springs up in gardens even after being cut down to ground level and can form a thick hedge. Unfortunately the Grootfontein nursery have very few to offer as seeds are hard to come by (due to the edible fruits) and seedlings are extremely slow growing.

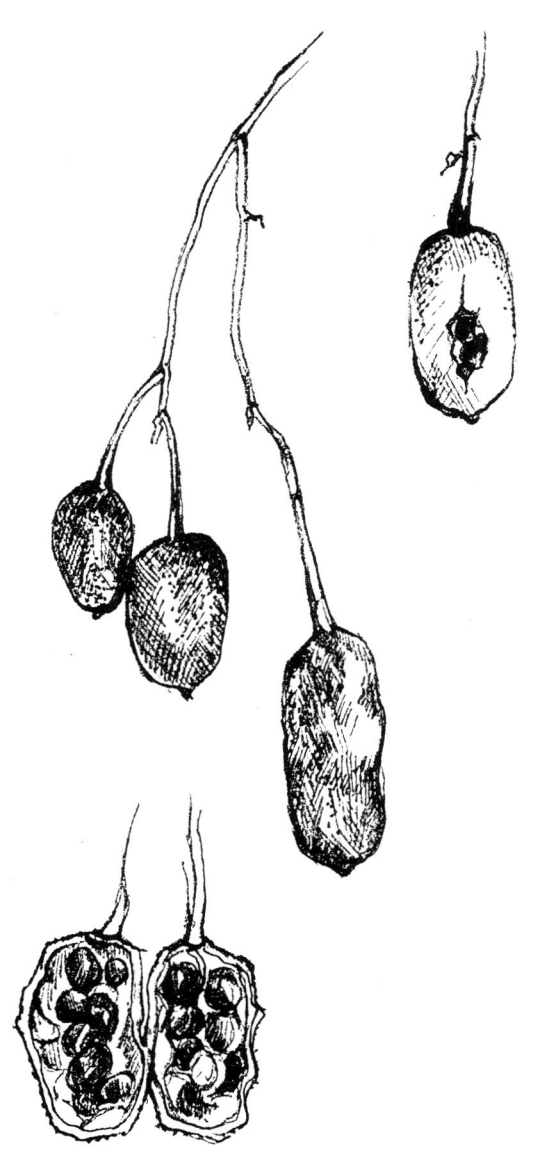

Acacia tortilis subsp. heteracantha 188

Umbrella thorn; krulpeul (Afrikaans); Ringelhülsenakazie (German); orusu orupunguya, (Herero)

Identification of this acacia is simple when pods are available, as no other species has such distinctively contorted pods. Another feature is the combination of long straight spines and short recurved ones. There are however two other acacia species at the Waterberg with this mixture – namely *Acacia luederitzii* and *Acacia reficiens*, but generally one thorn type will predominate on these trees e.g. short thorns are most common on the latter.

Acacia tortilis has many Owambo names and one assumes that it had uses that are no longer remembered. Other names relate to the pods, the two kinds of thorns or its shape. The word *tortilis* comes from the Latin for twisted and refers to the contorted or twisted pods, while the name for subspecies *heteracantha* comes from the Greek for "having different thorns". The characteristically flat-topped crown arising from a single stem is responsible for the name "umbrella thorn".

Acacia tortilis is a widespread tree found throughout Africa and Arabia and is divided into 4 subspecies, two of which occur at the Waterberg. The most commonly found subspecies – *heteracantha*, grows mainly in southern Africa while subsp. *spirocarpa* (a more hairy type) has a northerly distribution, reaching Ethiopia and Sudan and only as far south as the Waterberg in Namibia.

Acacia tortilis subsp. *heteracantha* can be found in the Transvaal, Natal and northern Cape. It does not occur in the south of this country and in the more arid areas it is noticeably smaller or a shrub and practically leafless for months. In other

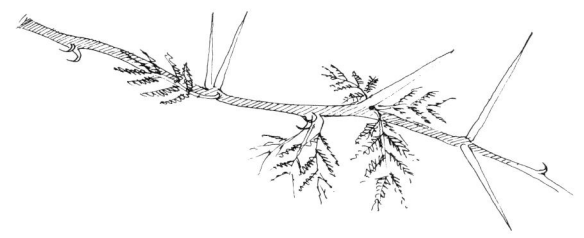

areas trees are reported to be leafless only after excessive cold or drought. Flowering probably takes place as a response to rain, with flowers in very pale yellow heads.

Small stock eat the fallen pods, while goats browse the lower branches occasionally. Pods are said to be highly nutritious, but at times may contain poisonous substances. Leaves and shoots are eaten by game and the branches by rhino. Wood is only used for fuel and branches for fencing. At times it exudes an edible gum. *Acacia tortilis* trees are favourite nesting places for birds like weavers, while the flat crown is a choice spot for the secretary bird. Seedlings are available from the Grootfontein nursery, but little is known about their progress. They make attractive trees in large gardens and where seedlings come up naturally, young plants grow very quickly, branching from the base and having many long white thorns.

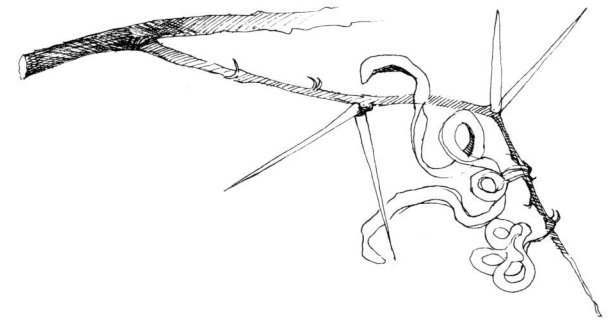

Acacia luederitzii var. *luederitzii* 174

False umbrella thorn; rooihaak (Afrikaans); Luderitzakazie (German); omungondo (Herero)

Acacia reficiens subsp. *reficiens* 181

Rooihaak (Afrikaans); Rotrindenakazie (German); omugondo (Herero)

Although the geographical ranges of these two species overlap at the Waterberg, it would appear that the distribution of the *Acacia luederitzii* stretches eastwards while the other westwards. They are very closely related differing in hairiness, the number of leaflets and pod size.

The local variety of *Acacia luederitzii*, namely var. *luederitzii* differs from that common in the Transvaal as it lacks swollen spines. Its bark has been used in Botswana for tanning skins, for arrow quivers and roofs of huts, while gum exuded by the tree is used to glue arrow shafts.

Acacia reficiens is more common in the drier western parts of Namibia, where it is usually a small, several-stemmed tree. The people of the Kaokoveld use the bark to curdle milk, the thorns to pierce ears and the branches for fencing. Leaves and pods are eaten by small stock.

FOREST WALK

Peltophorum africanum   215

Omuparara, weeping wattle, African wattle; huilboom, (Afrikaans); omuparara, also omuti (tree) wepaha (of the twins) (Herero)

Weeping wattle is an inappropriate name for this magnificent tree as wattles are becoming known as pests that encroach on the natural vegetation of our country and true wattles, with their fluffy mimosa-like flowers, come from Australia.

At first glance, especially at the leaves, the "omuparara" tree may be taken for an acacia or mimosa, but it has no thorns and belongs to a different legume sub-family. Regarding "weeping" trees, no records of this occurrence have been traced for this country. Perhaps the little bug *Ptyelus grossus* (a froghopper or spittlebug) responsible for the "tears", does not occur in our area.

The botanical name *Peltophorum* is derived from the Greek for "shield-bearing" and alludes either to the shield-like shape of the stigma or to the flat shield-like pods that it bears. The specific name *africana* (from Africa) refers to its distribution i.e. from southern Africa to central tropical Africa. It is very common in the Transvaal and also grows in Botswana, Swaziland and Natal. In Namibia, it occurs only in the northern areas and is one of the most characteristic trees of the Waterberg.

Peltophorum africanum may be small and branching from the base, or enormous as on the Forest Walk. It has a dense crown and rough dark bark. An important feature for identification is the stipule (i.e. a small modified leaf), that can only be seen on young growth. It is up to 1,4 cm long, has rust-coloured hairs and occurs on either side of the stem at the base of the leaf. Young branches are also covered with rust-coloured soft hairs. The bright, showy yellow flowers (up to 2 cm across) brighten up the veld in summer. These are followed by broad, flat pods that also decorate the tree for some time.

Leaves and side shoots are eaten by a variety of animals including elephant, giraffe and kudu. Whether or not the pods are eaten is debatable, but they are most certainly eaten by insects.

The gum exuded is reputed to be poisonous, but other parts of the tree are used medicinally throughout Africa. In Namibia,

a bark extract has been used by the Herero as a precaution against the birth of twins. A number of uses have been recorded from Owambo: kraals are built with branches; sticks are used for supporting large calabash butter churns; wood is made into handles for axes and hoes; cups and buckets are carved from the wood; and parts of the tree, ground up and mixed with water are applied to the hides of domestic animals as a repellent for flies whose maggots penetrate animal skins. Although dried roots can be used to poison food, pods mixed with baobab bark and a specific grass species are used as a magic cure for severe sickness.

Peltophorum africanum is a well-known garden plant in the Transvaal, where its "pleasing shape, soft feathery foliage and brilliant flowers are a delight to gardeners". Seedlings are available at the Grootfontein nursery and grow fairly fast in some parts of this country. It can stand a small amount of frost only and must be protected during its first winters.

The "huilboom" is protected in Namibia.

Combretum apiculatum

subsp. apiculatum 532

Kudu bush; koedoebos, koedoeboom (Afrikaans); Kudubusch (German); omumbuti (Herero)

subsp. leutweinii 532, 1

Hairy kudu bush; harige koedoebos (Afrikaans); omumbuti (Herero)

Anyone who knows the red bushwillow of the Transvaal or the large stands of shrubby kudu bush from other parts of Namibia, may wonder about this illustrated specimen. Not only is it a large single-stemmed tree, but the hairy leaves could almost be mistaken for those of the "appelblaar", especially when they are yellow and fall. However, as the name *apiculatum* implies, most of the leaf tips are apiculate i.e. they have short, sharp tips.

Two subspecies grow at the Waterberg with subsp. *apiculatum* occurring either as a tall tree or a shrub (on the Mountain View Walking Route), with noticeable insect galls. The tree in the painting is *Combretum apiculatum* subsp. *leutweinii* growing in close proximity to *Ficus sycomorus*.

Insect galls

Combretum apiculatum occurs as far north as Tanzania and Kenya. It also grows in Angola, Zambia, Mozambique, and Malawi. Subspecies *apiculatum* can be found in northern and central Namibia, as well as Botswana, the Transvaal, Natal, Swaziland, and Zimbabwe. Subspecies *leutweinii*, however is restricted to northern Namibia and a few isolated spots in Botswana. It was named after Theodor Leutwein, a German army officer and governor of German SWA from 1898 to 1905 who was keenly interested in the vegetation of the territory.

Leaves of *Combretum apiculatum* vary considerably in size, shape and position on the stem. The average leaf size is given as 7 by 4 cm, but they can be 2 to 14 cm long.

Although subsp. *leutweinii* is regarded as the hairy kudu bush, subsp. *apiculatum* may also have hairy leaves. However they are usually shiny, particularly when young, and may appear somewhat sticky. When hairs are present, they are either restricted to veins on the upper surface, or occur all over the lower surface. Hairy leaves are often on the same tree as smooth ones. Leaves of subsp. *leutweinii*, on the other hand, are never shiny or sticky, and although about the same length they are generally wider.

Sweet-smelling flowers occur any time from September to January, especially as a response to rain. They are small, greenish and about 25 are clustered in a 35 mm long spike. The 4-winged fruits are 2,5 cm long in both subspecies, initially yellowy-green and shiny, with the wings turning reddish and eventually yellow.

The leaves are eaten by a number of animals and farmers consider *Combretum apiculatum* a valuable fodder tree. Cattle seem to prefer the leaves when they are least nutritious i.e. when they are about to fall or are on the ground. Branches are eaten by rhino and elephant chew the bark. According to the Bushmen an edible gum is produced, but only rarely. In the Kaokoveld a medicinal powder is made from dry leaves and applied to the umbilical cord after childbirth. In areas where *Ficus glumosa* does not occur, an extract from the bark is used to tan leather.

Although the wood is tough, termite- and borer-proof, it is only used for fence posts and firewood, making excellent charcoal. In Owambo its main use is indicated by the name "stick-to-stir-porridge".

Combretum apiculatum is cultivated at the Grootfontein nursery and makes a suitable small tree for gardens, even in Windhoek, as it is frost and drought-resistant.

The name *Combretum* was given to a plant by Pliny who lived in the first century. Today over 200 species are known with about 20 in southern Africa. The genus is an important part of the Waterberg flora with some species being very common. They are not always easy to identify correctly without fruits.

Besides *Combretum imberbe* discussed on page 105, others at the Waterberg are:

Combretum collinum   541 which has a number of subspecies. The fruits are red-brown and up to 4 cm in diameter.

Combretum hereroense   538 with bright russet-red fruits, 2,5 cm long.

Combretum molle   537 – the velvet-leaf combretum, with fruit about 1,3 cm in diameter and reddish when mature.

Combretum psidioides subsp. *dinteri*   543,1 with drooping foliage and fruit 3 by 3 cm, a deep wine red colour.

Combretum zeyheri   546 with the largest combretum fruit, being up to 6 cm in diameter and light brown when mature.

KAMBAZEMBI WALKING ROUTE

Ficus cordata 51

Namaqua fig; Namakwavy (Afrikaans); Herzfeige (German); omukuumbwa, omumbaha, omukuju (Herero)

Along these Waterberg paths the tree with the greatest variety of forms is definitely *Ficus cordata.* It may be a tall erect tree, or a small plant coming out of a rock crevice with a most interesting shape.

Apart from this area, *Ficus cordata* grows in the drier regions of Namibia, Namaqualand, northern Cape and Botswana. Like all figs, it has milky latex and is often called

"melkboom" (milk-tree), however this is also the common name for a widespread tree *Sideroxylon inerme,* which does not occur in Namibia.

The leaves of *Ficus cordata* vary from 4 to 10 cm long and are always on long stalks. They generally taper to a sharp point, but the base is cordate or "heart-shaped" – hence the specific name. Ripe figs are less than a centimetre in diameter and purple with whitish specks. They are eaten by livestock, wild animals and birds, but not relished by humans. In the Kaokoveld the bark may be used for tanning skins. Leaves are also eaten by livestock.

Seedlings are available at the Grootfontein nursery and they grow into erect trees with smooth whitish trunks that are very attractive. They also make excellent bonzais.

Ficus cordata is protected in Namibia.

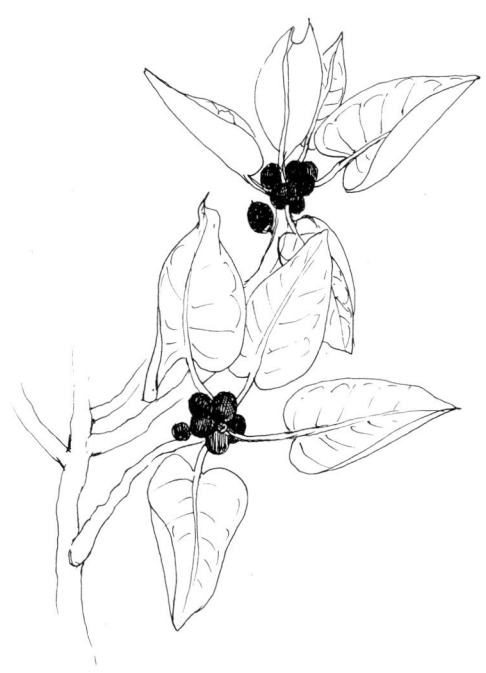

Obetia carruthersiana 69

Angola nettle; brandnetel (Afrikaans); Baumnessel (German)

Obetia carruthersiana belongs to the Urticaceae or Nettle family, so it is fortunate that these trees are off to one side of the Kambazembi Walking Route. They can also be seen along the Mountain View path.

Nettles are known for their stinging hairs and this plant is densely covered with long sharp hairs, occurring on twigs, leaves and stalks, especially new growth. The nettle hairs are long enough to be picked out, but as they are usually close together this may be difficult. The resulting burning sensation is rather uncomfortable for a time, depending on the sensitivity of ones skin.

The derivation of the name *Obetia* is not known, but the species was named after a British botanist W. Carruthers. It is the only *Obetia* in southern Africa and grows in the central and northern parts of Namibia and Angola.

Obetia carruthersiana may be a shrub with many branches from the base or a 6 m tall tree found on stony hills and mountain sides. Young twigs may be reddish and the leaves, which follow the flowers, have long, leafy persistent stipules. The leaves, which vary greatly in size (from 2,5 to 17 cm), are heart-shaped or lobed, have toothed margins and are on long stalks.

Male and female flowers are borne on different bushes. They are creamy-green and tiny, but occur in large numbers. The female flowers develop into small, dry fruits partially enclosed in the remains of the calyx.

Obetia carruthersiana belongs to a family of little economic importance, some species provide edible greens while another is a commercial soure of fiber.

Croton gratissimus 328

Apteek bossie, laventelkoorsbessie (Afrikaans); Lavendelbusch (German); omumbango, omumbangona [var. *subgratissimus*] (Herero)

Due to its wide distribution and many uses, *Croton gratissimus* has a number of common names often incorporating the word lavender, as the fragrant smell of crushed leaves is used as perfume. A direct translation of the botanical names means "the most pleasant tick of all". The word *Croton* comes from the Greek for 'tick', probably a reference to the seeds and *gratissimus* is derived from the Latin for 'pleasant'.

Croton gratissimus grows from the RSA, through Botswana, Zimbabwe, Zambia and Mozambique to tropical Africa. In Namibia it occurs throughout the northern parts.

Croton plants growing along the path between the camp site and the Rasthaus, are usually shrubs less than a metre high. Those found along the Kambazembi Walking Route or en route to the plateau are trees a few metres tall and in the tropics they reach 8 m. It is easy to recognize *Croton gratissimus* however, as the leaves are very distinctive and attractive. The dark green upper surfaces set off the silvery lower surfaces of the leaves whose glands are seen as reddish-brown dots. Occasionally a leaf may be yellow or orange. These colour combinations are eye-catching, especially in bright sunshine.

The small flowers are either male or female and they occur on the same stalk. They result in a 3-lobed fruit.

It is perhaps not surprising that parts of this plant are reputed to be poisonous, as the *Croton* genus (which includes about

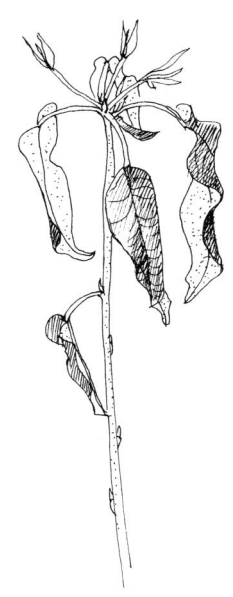

700 species) belongs to the Euphorbiaceae family – known for its variety of succulents and toxic milky sap. Nevertheless the leaves of *Croton gratissimus* are browsed by small stock in the Kaokoveld. Wood is used to carve knobkerries and walking sticks and in Owambo knobkerries carved from this wood are used mainly for special ceremonies. Dolls are also carved from croton wood with a mixture of clay and beeswax being used for certain parts.

The fruits are eaten by a variety of birds and some butterflies are associated with these trees. The leaves are crushed for perfume and also used as a love charm. There are also a number of medicinal uses and one Zulu name means "that which strikes at sickness".

Croton gratissimus has been successfully grown in Grootfontein nursery and it makes a most attractive ornamental shrub/tree for the garden. It is fairly fast growing, but needs protection from frost when young.

One mistletoe seen at the Waterberg, *Tapinanthus glaucocarpus* grows mainly on *Croton* trees.

Securinega virosa 309

White-berry bush; witbessiebos (Afrikaans); Schneebeeren-busch (German); omutaareka (Herero)

Strangely enough another shrub growing along these paths belonging to the Euphorbiaceae family, has a specific name referring to its unpleasant smelling leaves – it is *Securinega virosa*

This is a very widely distributed plant growing from Africa to Asia. It is obvious at certain times of the year, in particular when bearing the waxy white berries (about 5 mm in diam.) responsible for the common name. Only some bushes bear these fruits as the tiny male and female flowers are borne on different plants.

Leaves are browsed by antelope and livestock. The wood is said to be very strong and is used for fencing posts. It has been grown as a hedge in some countries. Seedlings are available at the Grootfontein nursery, but details on growth in Namibia are still unavailable.

Lonchocarpus nelsii 239

Appelblaar (Afrikaans); Apfelblatt (German); omupanda (Herero)

This is certainly one of the loveliest trees of the northern areas of this country. Fairly common beside the main roads, especially in the Otjiwarongo district, Lonchocarpus nelsii seems to occur north of a line connecting Omaruru with the Waterberg. It continues into the Caprivi Strip, Angola, Botswana, Zimbabwe and Zambia.

The botanical name is based on the Greek words for "lance-shaped fruit" while the species is named after Nels, a plant collector in this country in the 1880's who assisted Dr. Heinrich Goering (father of Field Marshal Goering) when he was Reichs Commissioner for German SWA.

The stiff leaves, reminiscent of those of the apple tree, are responsible for the common name "appelblaar" (apple leaf). When young they are very hairy, but by maturity (about 10 cm long and 5-6 cm wide), they are less so. These leaves turn yellow in winter and are a conspicuous sight, both on the tree

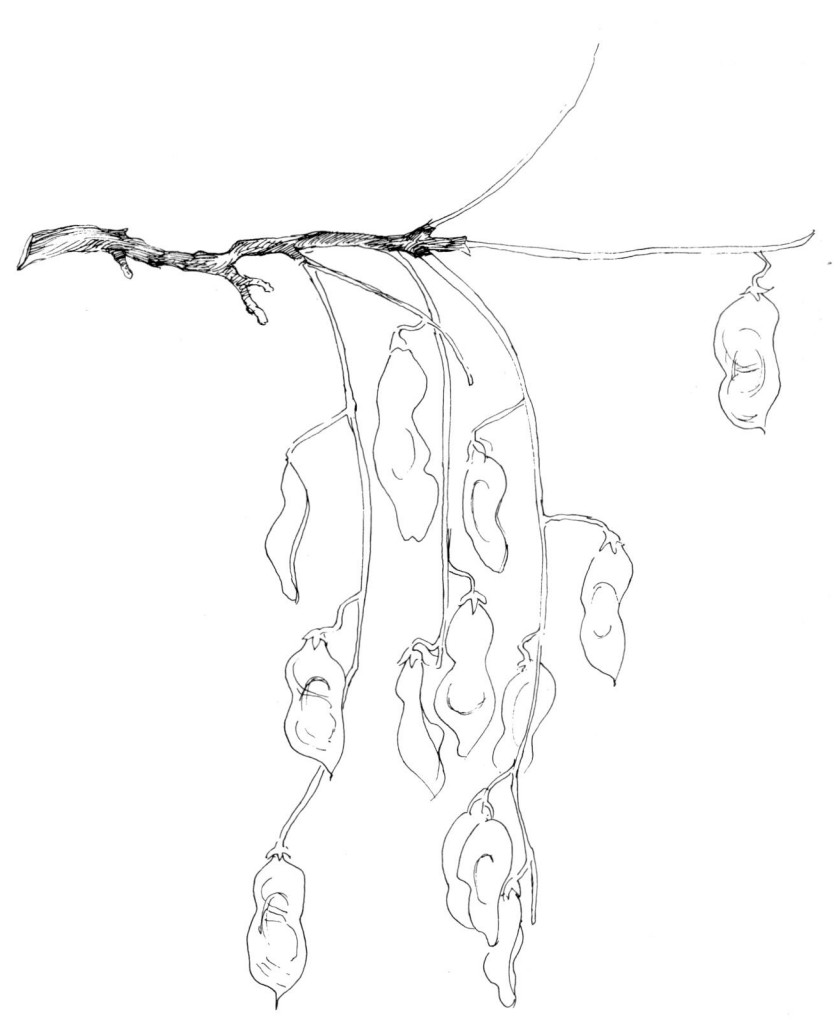

and as a yellow carpet below them. After dropping, sprays of lavender-blue flowers take over, attracting hundreds of eager insects. In some years and on certain trees, the flowers are noticeably less striking in colour and may even be missed if one passes at speed on the main road, however these peashaped flowers are definitely worth a closer look.

Lonchocarpus nelsii, a legume of subfamily Papilionoideae, has pods that are 4 to 7 cm long, flattish and papery. For a short period when these finely haired, pale green pods are young and abundant the tree takes on yet another colour.

Fallen flowers are utilized by dik-dik, as well as insects. Pods are eaten by black-faced impala, and the leaves by horses and stock. At the Waterberg eland eat fallen leaves in dry periods i.e. June to August.

In the Kaokoveld the scaly outer bark is scraped off and put into milk to promote curdling, while spoons are carved from the wood. The Bushmen are said to use the wood as stamper or scraper handles and the Heikum Bushmen drink a cooked bark mixture as cough medicine. The leaves are also used as a covering for boils or sores. In Owambo tree trunks provide sitting places for guests or family gatherings around the fire.

Seedlings are available from the nursery in Grootfontein. They transplant well, but grow slowly initially and must be protected from frost when young.

This tree is protected in Namibia.

Commiphora tenuipetiolata 289

Satin-bark commiphora; witstamkanniedood (Afrikaans)

The commiphora said to have the most beautiful bark of all is *Commiphora tenuipetiolata*. The latter name being derived from the fact that the petioles or leaf stalks are very thin.

It grows in the northern parts of Namibia and to a limited extent in the Transvaal and Zimbabwe. It can be a bush or a tree, 2 to 12 metres tall. The leaves have either 3 leaflets or 2 to 4 pairs of leaflets plus a terminal one. Male and female flowers are borne on separate plants and they result in roundish fruits over one cm in diameter and dark red when ripe. The fleshy parts split to expose the stone which has a thin fleshy outer covering called a pseudaril. In this species it covers about two-thirds of the stone.

When leafless, which is most of the year, some commiphora species are difficult to tell apart. The most reliable feature for identification purposes is the pseudaril, but as these are often brightly coloured and attractive to birds, they are not readily available.

A similar species, but one that is generally more shrub-like, with hairy leaves is *Commiphora angolensis* (no. 272). Called "omuhangorwa" or "omongorwa" in Herero, it also has a flaking bark. The wood is used in Kaokoveld and Owambo for carved household utensils and its tuber can be eaten like a carrot. It is widely distributed in northern Namibia and also grows in the Transvaal, Botswana, Angola, Malawi, Zambia and Zimbabwe.

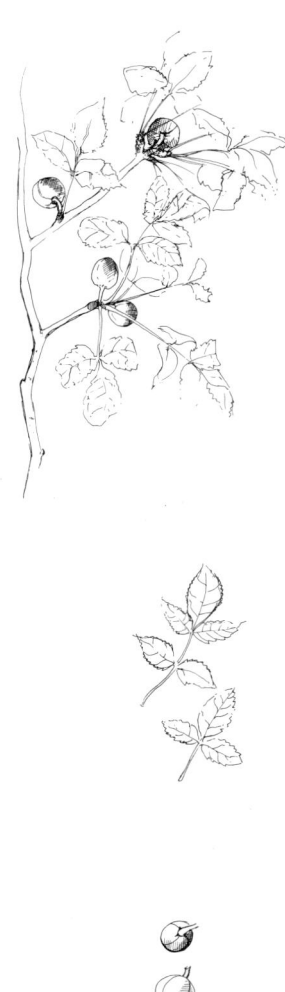

Acacia hereroensis   171

Bergdoring (Afrikaans); Bergdorn (German); oroo (Herero)

Although the botanical name of this tree indicates that it flourishes in Hereroland in Namibia, it can be found from Grootfontein in the north to Karasberg in the south. It frequents mountainous regions and is particularly common in the Windhoek area. It also grows in the Transvaal, OFS and Cape and to a limited extent in Botswana and Zimbabwe. In some areas it is labelled "dolomite thorn" because of its preference for this soil type.

The trees along the Kambazembi Walking Route are erect and a few metres tall, but in other districts *Acacia hereroensis* grows as a bushy shrub. The name "rooihaak" (red thorn), used in the RSA, comes from the colour of thorns on young growth. Other thorns are however much darker, they are also particularly sharp and short and break off easily.

The leaves of this acacia are very fine, nevertheless different forms are found over its range. Flowering time varies and may take place after rain, usually the tree already has leaves. The flowers, in a 70 mm long spike, are cream or white and scented. They have been used in a cough mixture.

In late autumn when this painting was done the pods, being abundant and straw to ginger-coloured, were eye-catching. The pods are straight, 100 mm long and about 15 mm wide, with minor constrictions between the seeds.

These attractive and shady trees are relatively drought-resistant and have been propagated successfully in some areas.

Dombeya rotundifolia   471

Wild pear; dikbas (Afrikaans); Südwester Schneeballstrauch (German); omuryahere (Herero)

The Swazi people have given this tree a very apt name – "the tree that heralds the new season". But like many widespread plants *Dombeya rotundifolia* has a number of other common names. Most of these are derived from the wonderful show of flowers that announce spring-time. To many, they resemble pear blossoms and in some areas it is known as the blossom tree.
    The botanical name comes from an eighteenth century French botanist, Joseph Dombey who travelled in Peru and Chile. The species name *rotundifolia* is the Latin for "having round leaves".
    The variety of *Dombeya rotundifolia* growing at the Waterberg, occurs from the Rehoboth area to the northern parts of Namibia. It does not grow in the very dry regions of the country, except on mountain ranges e.g. the Brandberg. It can also be found in Botswana, the Transvaal, Swaziland, Natal and northwards to tropical east Africa. A different variety is found in the Naukluft Mountains of Namibia.
    The wild pear is usually a shrub or small tree in this country, but in other regions of Africa it can reach 10 m. The masses of creamy-white flowers may be seen as early as July. The petals then become papery and fade to a cinnamon or brownish colour and act as wings to the fruit. Both stages are very attractive. The new leaves that appear after the flowers are almost circular and vary from 2,5 to 8 cm long, but in tropical areas may be 15 cm in diam. Like most members of the Sterculiaceae family, short star-shaped hairs can be seen on both surfaces under a microscope. These are responsible for the rough texture.
    The wild pear is utilized by many animals. Kudu browse the leaves and young shoots and insects are attracted to it. It is used extensively as medicine, for magic and as a love potion. Early writers like Galpin reported that the wood was excellent, for example as mine props, but as it is much smaller in our country compared to the tropics, it has not been used to the same extent. The strong bark fibre is used to make rope.

Dombeya rotundifolia grows easily and fairly quickly and is a pleasing garden plant. It withstands light frost and is fire-resistant. It is available at the Grootfontein nursery.

Osyris lanceolata 100

Bergbas (Afrikaans)

This shrub is not spectacular, common at the Waterberg or beneficial, but it is interesting. It belongs to the Santalaceae or sandalwood family that is widely distributed over the whole world. This family includes many parasites and although not all species have been investigated, it is suspected that they may all be parasitic. A report of *Osyris lanceolata* from Zimbabwe, dating back many years, indicated that it could be a root parasite. Thus as it is evergreen, it would only need to obtain supplies of water and minerals from its host.

Osyris lanceolata grows in the central parts of this country, the Cape, OFS, the Transvaal and Lesotho to tropical Africa. The botanical name *Osyris* is based on the Latin word for "branch", a reference to the numerous branches. While the specific name refers to the lance-shaped leaves.

It is a hardy evergreen tree or large shrub with rather rigid branches. The dull leaves are leathery, 1,3 to 5 cm long and have pointed tips. Like most plants in this family the flowers are small, rather inconspicuous and pollinated by a variety of insects. In this species the greenish male and female flowers occur on separate bushes. The fruits are green at first, becoming yellow, then orange and red and are attractive to some birds.

The common name in the RSA "looibos" (tan bush) comes from the use the Voortrekkers had for this bush i.e. tanning. In North Africa the wood is sometimes used as a substitute for sandalwood.

Ficus ilicina 53

Laurel fig; klimvy rotsvy (Afrikaans); Kletterfeige (German); omupendarwa (Herero)

In contrast to the other two figs at the Waterberg, *Ficus ilicina* is never an erect tree. Its white stem spreads sideways and the exposed roots clasp the rocks over which they grow.

A feature, shared by about 900 other species of *Ficus*, is the "fruit" or fig which in fact is not a fruit at all, but a receptacle whose inner walls are lined with hundreds of minute flowers. These flowers may be male, female or infertile female flowers. They are pollinated by wasps and each species has its own pollinating wasp.

In Namibia, *Ficus ilicina* was previously known as *Ficus guerichiana*, being named after Prof. Georg Gürich, a German geologist, who collected plants in this country around 1888. Its distribution is more limited than the other two found at the Waterberg, being mainly concentrated in the drier western parts of Namibia. It also grows in the south west Cape (from Clanwilliam northwards) and Angola.

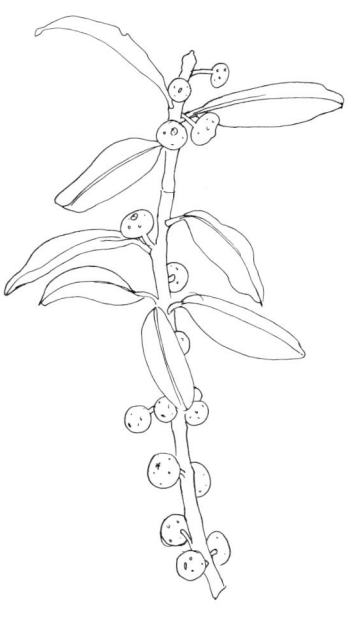

Recognition of *Ficus ilicina* from afar is not difficult as its slender, but thick leaves are crowded at the tips of the branches making a dense and obvious mass of green on rocky cliffs, hills and mountains.

The pea-sized figs are roundish and slightly hairy with a pore at the end. They are only consumed by humans in times of need, but many animals and birds eat them.

Kirkia acuminata   267

Bergsering (Afrikaans); Bergsyringe, (German); omuhoho (Herero)

Dr. John Kirk explorer, naturalist and for a time a companion of Dr. David Livingstone was the first to collect this tree and it was given his name. It belongs to the Simaroubaceae family, probably only known in southern Africa for an exotic that is sometimes cultivated called the "tree of Heaven".

As the Afrikaans name "bergsering" (mountain seringa) implies, *Kirkia acuminata* generally occurs on rocky hills where its spreading crown resembles a seringa. It is conspicuous in the northern parts of Namibia, but infrequent in this part of the Waterberg Park. A few are found in northern Botswana and it is fairly common in Zimbabwe and tropical Africa. In the northern Transvaal it is called the "white seringa".

The bark has been made into rope in the Kaokoveld and in Zimbabwe the fibres are woven into material. The swollen roots are said to store liquid and can quench thirst in times of drought.

Although furniture can be made from it, which is both beautiful and unusual, it is not considered durable or profitable as silica crystals found in the wood blunt saws and equipment.

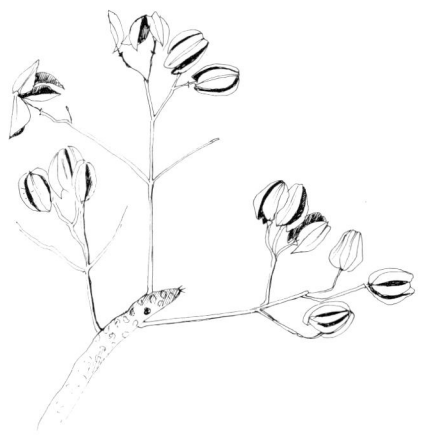

Kirkia acuminata grows easily from seed or truncheons and makes a fine deciduous tree for gardens. It is fairly fast-growing and drought-resistant, but susceptible to frost and must be protected when young. In parts of Zimbabwe it is regarded as a sacred tree and in Namibia it is protected.

Steganotaenia araliacea 569

Carrot tree; geelwortelboom (Afrikaans); Wilder Selleriebaum (German); omutiwonyoka, epondo (Herero)

At times the light green-grey trunks of this very interesting tree are obvious against the scree and can be recognized from the bungalows. They occur just before reaching the top of the Mountain View Route and a few grow on the Kambazembi Walking Route.

The botanical name comes from the Greek *steganos* meaning "covered" and Latin *taenia* for a band – the inference being unclear. The specific name is derived from the genus *Aralia* which it resembles. It belongs to an economically important family providing food, condiments and ornamentals that are characteristically aromatic. Examples are carrots, parsnip, celery and parsely, and plants used for flavouring like anise, caraway, dill and fennel.

Steganotaenia araliacea is one of the few trees in this family and it has no close relatives in Namibia. It is confined to the northern parts of this country, but also occurs in the Transvaal, Botswana, Angola, Zimbabwe and Mozambique, extending northwards to central tropical Africa.

The small yellowy-green flowers of the carrot tree appear in spring in umbels. The Latin word "umbrella" means sunshade,

and this collection of flowers does resemble just that — spokes and all! The tree is usually leafless when in flower or in fruit and makes an attractive sight. The fruits are straw-coloured and about 8 mm long and succeeded by fine foliage, crowded at the ends of branches. The compound leaves are about 30 cm long, with 2 to 4 pairs of leaflets and a terminal one. They have conspicuously toothed margins and end in a fine hair-like point.

In the Kaokoveld the straight stems of *Steganotaenia araliacea* are used for making sacred fire sticks which are the only means whereby the sacred fire may be kindled. In other areas the tree is used for medicinal purposes — sore throats are relieved by chewing roots and parts of the bark alleviate asthma. In Zimbabwe children make pop-guns by slipping the bark off a length of stem, this bark comes away easily in late winter.

Carrot trees grow well and strongly if not over-watered. The rate of growth varies, but as the bark is decorative and it flowers (even while still young), it is recommended for gardens. It is available at the Grootfontein nursery.

MOUNTAIN VIEW WALKING ROUTE
Erythrina decora 243

Coral tree; Namibkoraalboom (Afrikaans); Korallenbaum (German); omuṇi, omuṇinga (tree), oṇinga (fruit) (Herero)

No matter how daunting the walk to the plateau may seem, a chance to see *Erythrina decora* in flower should not be missed. Fortunately these trees occur below the summit, they grow beside the path and the walk is not too strenuous.

Although there are about 100 species of *Erythrina* in the world, this country's one indigenous coral tree has a botanical name meaning "the lovely erythrina". As flowering usually takes place in spring before the leaves appear it is an eye-catching sight. It grows in rocky localities in central and northern Namibia only and is not very common.

The other *Erythrina* found in northern Namibia is also indigenous, but is a suffrutex i.e. it has large tuberous roots that annually give rise to slender above-ground shoots.

The name *Erythrina* is derived from the Greek word *erythros* meaning red, a reference to the flowers, which have 5 petals — one large and conspicuous. The buds of the local *Erythrina*, being silver and velvety, are very distinct. They open into flowers arranged in a dense cluster that is about 9 cm long. Pods become woody with age and being constricted between the bulging seeds, appear like a string of beads. They are slightly hairy, 10 cm long and 1,3 cm wide and split to show scarlet and black seeds.

Erythrina decora can be a small shrubby tree with pale stems or erect specimens with dark trunks sometimes 9 m tall. The branches and twigs are prickly and young twigs, like the buds and young leaves, are densely covered with silver-white velvety hairs. The leaves vary considerably in size with leaflets from 3 to 5 cm broad to ones of 14 to 18 cm broad.

The bright red seeds of *Erythrina* species are well known as "lucky beans" and have been used by many people for "lucky" necklaces and bracelets. They are also considered poisonous, but according to research that has been done on about 50 species, they are unlikely to harm, unless crushed and injected into tissue. However they must never be mistaken for the dangerous seeds of *Abrus precatorius*, a wild plant of the same family.

The only use recorded for these seeds in Namibia, comes from the Kaokoveld. Here seeds, are used to decorate a type of trumpet (made from gemsbok horn and beeswax) which is used to keep herds of stock together.

Recent studies by the CSIR and the University of Cape Town have discovered a substance in *Erythrina caffra* that may be valuable in the treatment of patients with coronary or other thromboses. A similar substance has been discovered in *Erythrina decora*.

Depending on the availability of seeds, plants can be bought from the Grootfontein nursery and they do very well. A coral tree grows at the Camp site, which perhaps due to watering, appears to flower before the wild specimens. It is a protected tree in Namibia.

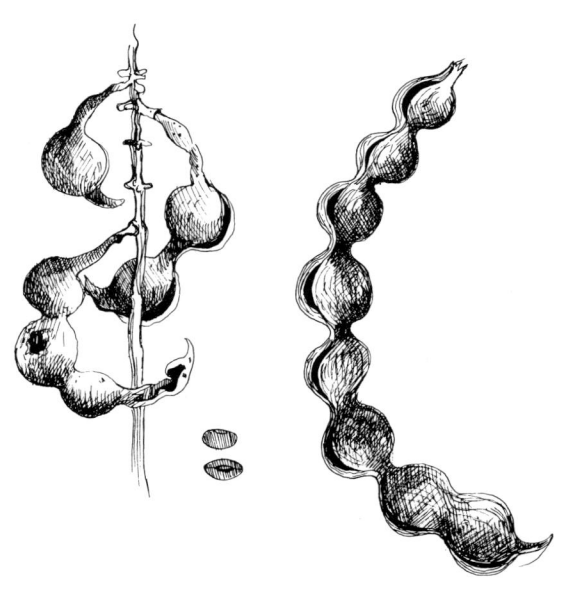

FIG TREE WAY

Ficus sycomorus   66

Sycamore fig, common cluster fig; wildevy (Afrikaans); Sykomore (German); omukuyu (tree) omakuyu (fruit) (Herero)

This fig tree, one of the largest in southern Africa and probably the most widely distributed fig, is the sycomore of the Bible. The Greek word *sycomorus* literally means fig-mulberry, the latter being the family to which it belongs.

Ficus sycomorus occurs naturally in the savannas of southern Arabia and in eastern and southern Africa. Besides this country, it is found in Natal, the Transvaal, Botswana, Mozambique, Zimbabwe, Zambia and Angola. In the Middle East where it was introduced centuries ago, it is still being cultivated today for fruit and timber. These sycamores must be cultivated from cuttings, as seeds are not produced. Probably its specific pollinating wasp has been unable to reach this region.

Ficus sycomorus grows well on river banks or areas with a high water-table. In southern Africa these trees grow to about 30 m tall, while in tropical Africa they can reach 46 m. The big leaves (7 to 10 cm by 5 to 7 cm) are characterized by being very rough. Ripe figs, are yellowish or pinkish and about 2,5 cm in diameter. They usually occur in dense clusters on the main branches and trunk, often more than once a year.

Although nothing like as tasty as cultivated figs and usually full of insects, these are the largest and sweetest of the indigenous figs. They are eaten fresh or dried for later use. In Owambo they are sometimes cooked in water, allowed to ferment and distilled as brandy ("olambika"). Both wild animals and domestic stock enjoy the fruits. Cattle are said to pick the ripest, while even fish eat fallen fruits. Birds including hornbills and rollers enjoy figs.

In the Kaokoveld goats are fond of the leaves, thus the trees often have a noticable browse line. They are highly nutritious and useful fodder. In some areas, concoctions of the leaves, bark and latex are used to treat a variety of ailments.

In the past the bark was used for tanning and dyeing skins. Sticks were rubbed together to generate fire and the wood was used for making drums. Mummy cases found intact after several thousands of years in Eygpt are reputed to be of this wood.

A large tree would probably need a garden to itself, but seedlings are available at Grootfontein nursery. It can grow from cuttings made from the previous year's growth and is relatively fast growing.

Ficus sycomorus is protected in Namibia.

Rhus lancea   386

Karee (Afrikaans); Sumach (German); oruso, ousauroro (fruit) (Herero)

Rhus species in Africa are characterized by having leaves with 3 leaflets usually arising from one point i.e. palmately trifoliate. Identification using this feature is fairly easy at the Waterberg unlike habit or shape which vary considerably.

The name *rhus* is apparently derived from the Greek *rhous* meaning red and given to a small tree in the mango family, whose bark and fruit were used in tanning. *Lancea* refers to the "lance-shaped" leaves. Altogether there are over 250 *Rhus* species with about 60 occuring in southern Africa. Some have pleasant tasting fruit and are known as wild currants, while others are called karees. This word is derived from the

Hottentot word on which the name "karoo" is based and was first recorded as far back as 1778.

Rhus lancea is one of the best known karees because of its very wide distribution. In Namibia it grows from the Waterberg to the Orange River and practically throughout southern Africa (except Natal). In drier areas it is usually confined to stream banks and watercourses.

The foliage, which is droopy and willow-like, may be shed in late spring at the same time that new leaves are forming, thus it appears to be evergreen. The leaves, about 13 cm long, are made up of 3 long narrow pointed leaflets that are dark green and shiny above, but paler below. The minute flowers are yellow-green and are sometimes so abundant that the trees take on a yellowish tinge. Male and female flowers are found on different plants, thus fruits will only occur on some trees. They are small and roundish, with a brown outer skin.

All parts of *Rhus lancea* have been used in some way or other. The fruits, although not particularly tasty can be eaten. In some areas they are pounded with water and fermented to make a beer. Birds eat them and they make excellent poultry food. The foliage is browsed and flowers are utilized by many kinds of insects. The bark was once used for tanning. The wood is hard, tough, durable, close-grained, rather splintery and red-brown in colour. It works and polishes well and has a pleasant smell when fresh. Wagon parts, flooring and furniture were made from large logs and it was also used extensively for fence posts and tool handles. Supple branchlets were used by Bushmen to make bows.

The karee grows easily from seed or cuttings and progresses fairly fast for an indigenous plant. Gardeners have a choice of tidier male trees or female ones with fruit that attract birds. It is drought- and termite-resistent and does well on a variety of soils. It can be trained to be a single stemmed shade tree or trimmed for hedges. It is available at many local nurseries and is protected in Namibia.

Rhus marlothii   389, 2

Bitterkaree (Afrikaans); okaryangwari, okasauroro (Herero)

Named after the noted Cape botanist Rudolf Marloth, the bitter karee is found mainly in Namibia, but also occurs in the Transvaal and Botswana.

The part of the plant responsible for the common name bitter karee is unclear. It probably applies to the leaves as they are not grazed by stock, while the fruits are chewed to quench thirst. At the Waterberg it is utilized by eland in early spring. As it is evergreen, it may be eaten because it is available, rather than because it is tasty. *Rhus marlothii* is less distinctive than *Rhus lancea* and at the Waterberg is either a shrub or small tree often clumped with other plants. Some grow near the *Osyris* which was painted along the Kambazembi Walking Route.

Two other *Rhus* species found at the Waterberg are:
Rhus tenuinervis   393,2 the Kalahari currant, with softly leathery leaves that are hairy and red in winter.
Rhus ciliata, a small shrub, therefore without a tree number is locally called the fire bush as its evergreen foliage is ideal for fire-fighting in winter.

Ziziphus mucronata 447

Buffalo thorn; blinkblaar-wag-'n-bietjie (Afrikaans); Wart-ein-bisschen (German); omukaru, ozongaru (Herero)

In the dry season *Ziziphus mucronata* is not always as shiny as the common name "blinkblaar" (shiny leaf), would suggest. However a close encounter will leave one in no doubt about the validity of the "wag-'n-bietjie" or "wait-a-bit" section. Its spines are either recurved or straight and are strong and extremely sharp. In the past farmers used branches for building kraals to protect domestic stock and themselves from wild animals, including buffalo – hence the common name buffalo thorn.

The generic name is derived from the Arabic word *zizouf* and first given to a plant in that area. Other well-known *Ziziphus* species include the jujube and *Ziziphus spina-christi* from which Christ's crown of thorns is said to have been made. The latter apparently resembles *Ziziphus mucronata,* whose specific name, meaning 'pointed' in Latin, refers to the thorns.

Ziziphus mucronata is a widely distributed tree having no "typical" shape, as it grows in such a variety of habitats. It occurs throughout this country, in the RSA, Botswana, Swaziland, Mozambique as well as northwards to Ethiopia and Arabia.

The foliage, which is glossy, is irregularly deciduous, so that along these Waterberg paths one may see rather sparsely leafed trees and other very lush shiny ones. The small flowers are very attractive to insects and bee keepers like these trees. The fruits, often no bigger than a pea, are reddish brown when ripe with a fairly leathery skin and a thin layer of pulp surrounding a seed. Although the fruits are not widely eaten by humans because of the rather acrid taste, they are a very important source of food for a great variety of animals – birds, monkeys, warthogs, impala, nyala, black rhino, rats, mice and giraffe. Strangely, the fruit is sometimes regarded as poisonous in tropical Africa, however in different parts of southern Africa, it is used as a cure for a variety of ailments.

In the Kaokoveld the berries are eaten fresh, but dried ones are preferred. These may be mixed with meal or porridge. In Owambo wine is fermented and sometimes the fruits are distilled to make a strong brandy. In times of need i.e. during the Anglo-Boer War seeds were used as a coffee substitute. It is said that ground roots can be used in the same way. In Owambo

a decoction made from the leaves is used to treat fever (e.g. malaria), sore eyes or diarrhoea in children. Roots are used in the treatment of dysentery.

The wood is used in the Kavango for building houses and in Owambo for tool handles and whip-sticks. Previously yokes, yoke-pins and wagon shafts were made from it. Leaves are browsed by domestic stock and wild animals and the tree is considered valuable fodder. In the Waterberg, dry leaves are eaten from the ground by eland. In some parts the presence of this tree is believed to indicate underground water, while in other regions, it is said to ward off lightning.

Seedlings of *Ziziphus mucronata,* which are available at the Grootfontein nursery, grow fairly quickly and can withstand intense heat and cold. They grow in many different soil types and are drought-resistant. If trimmed they make good security hedges.

ANT HILL WAY

Dichrostachys cinerea subsp. africana 190

Sickle bush, Kalahari Christmas tree; sekelbos, omatjette (Afrikaans); Farbkätzchenstrauch (German); omutjete (Herero)

The Greek word *Dichrostachys* meaning two-coloured, points to the attractive pink and yellow flowers of this plant. As they often occur in December, it may be called the Kalahari Christmas tree. In other areas it is referred to as the Chinese lantern tree because of the hanging flowers. The name sickel bush is derived from the shape of the pods, while a less complimentary, but very apt name used in Namibia is "papwielbos" (flat-tyre bush) because of the sharp thorns.
 Dichrostachys cinerea is found in Africa, India and Australia, but subspecies *africana* is restricted to the northern and central parts of Namibia, Botswana, Transvaal, Swaziland and Natal.
 The leaves are very similar to those of Acacias, but the sickle bush is easily differentiated from them by its thorns and the colours of the flowers. The thorns are actually short, sharp side shoots that may bear leaves. The flower spikes can be 2,5 to 12 cm long, with tiny yellow fertile flowers in the upper part and sterile pink or purple flowers below.
 Dichrostachys cinerea grows in a very wide range of habitats and varies considerably. In many parts of this country, it is rapidly encroaching onto disturbed areas, particularly when over-grazed. Nevertheless, it makes excellent fire-wood and has other uses. In Kavango wood has been used for knobkerries and building kraals and in Owambo archery bows are made from it.
 Pods have a high protein content and are eaten by various species of game, from dik-dik to kudu and eland. Rhino and giraffe eat the leaves and shoots.

Different parts of the sickel bush are used to some extent in African medicine. Leaves and roots are chewed to produce a kind of local anaesthesia, useful in the treatment of conditions like snake-bite and sore eyes.

Combretum imberbe   539

Omumborombonga, leadwood; hardekool (Afrikaans); Ahnenbaum, (German); omumborombonga (Herero)

Although occurring from the Transvaal to tropical Africa, some of the most magnificent *Combretum imberbe* trees grow in Namibia. Here they have played an important part in the history of the Herero and Owambo people and this is reflected in the common name "Ahnenbaum". This refers to the belief that it is the ancestral tree from which came the first people, cattle, sheep and wild animals.

Other common names refer either to the hard charcoal that the tree yields after burning – "hardekool", or to the heaviness of the wood – "leadwood". The Guinness Book of Records (1984) gives *Olea capensis* subsp. *marcrocarpa* – the Ironwood (ysterhout) of the evergreen forests of RSA as the heaviest wood in the whole world, however, according to the Dendrological Society of SA, if one considers average density, the leadwood would be the real record holder. Its wood has an average density of 1180 kg/m^3, while that of the ironwood is only 1020 kg/m^3. Because of the hardness of the wood, dead trees can remain standing for years and some living trees have large dead branches. Certain "omumborombonga" may also be among the oldest of trees. Carbon dating carried out in Swaziland, has given ages of over a thousand years for *Combretum imberbe* trees.

The word *imberbe* comes from the Latin for "beardless" and probably refers to the leaves that have no hairs. They are relatively small for Combretums, 38 by 18 mm on average, but can be 8 cm long. Characteristics that are more valuable for identification purposes are: the white or grey bark which is cracked into small pieces, the size of the tree (up to 21 m, but usually 6 to 14 m) and the spiny young growth.

The 4-winged fruits that are about 15 by 15 mm, are greenish-yellow, but turn biscuit-coloured when ripe. They are densely clustered along the stems, giving the trees a yellowish tinge at times.

Combretum imberbe exudes edible gum infrequently. Its leaves are browsed by kudu and other antelope, while giraffe and elephants eat the leaves and branches. Bushmen and Damara inhale burnt leaves to treat colds and coughs and in other areas a cough mixture is prepared from the flowers. In

Owambo, medicine obtained from the root is used for stomach-ache.

In days gone by hoes, sleepers, fencing posts and mine props were made from the wood. In Owambo the coals were put in flat-irons and the stems used in the construction of kraal fences and huts. Wood ash is said to make good whitewash.

Today this tree is fortunately protected by forestry laws as its usefulness, especially as fuel, has resulted in a drastic decline in numbers.

Although considered to be extremely slow-growing because of the hardness of the wood, varying rates of growth have been recorded from the RSA. It is a good shade tree and is termite-resistant, but must be protected from frost when young. Seedlings are available at the Grootfontein nursery.

Euclea undulata 601, 1

Guarri; ghwarrie (Afrikaans); Bergebenholzstrauch, Feuerbusch (German); omukarambandje, omusema, muthime (Herero)

Euclea undulata has wavy or undulating leaves in the area where it was first collected, hence the name *undulata*. However over its wide range this feature is not constant and two varieties are recognized, with variety *myrtina* in Namibia. At the Waterberg an extreme form is found, making the specific name even less appropriate. Here the leaves are larger and have flatter margins. They are also more yellow-green and leathery. The botanical name *euclea* is based on the Greek word for glory or fame.

Euclea undulata is a twiggy evergreen shrub, forming clumps along some of the paths. In Namibia, it occurs from the Waterberg to the south of the country. It also grows in the Cape, the Transvaal, Natal, Botswana, Swaziland and sporadically in Zimbabwe. Male and female flowers are found on separate plants and both are very small, greeny-white in colour and fragrant. In the Cape honey made from the nectar of the flowers is called "ghwarriheuning" (guarri honey).

The berries are fleshy and red, turning purple or black when ripe. According to Burchell, who discovered this species in about 1811, these berries were among the few edible fruits available in Botswana. "Ghwarribessies" were also mentioned by Thunberg in 1771. He recorded that the Hottentots ate the berries or left them to ferment producing a kind of vinegar. The fruits are not very tasty, but are utilized by many animals, particularly mousebirds, white-crowned shrikes and baboon. The leaves are also browsed by stock and kudu.

The root is chewed by Heikum Bushmen for toothache. It has a sharp, medicinal taste that burns the mouth for a few hours. In other areas powdered root is used as a purgative. The wood, which is said to contain tannin was used for joinery and is also suitable for fencing posts.

Euclea undulata is fairly slow-growing, but can be used for hedges and is available at the Grootfontein nursery. When established it requires little water and makes a good evergreen, frost-resistant shrub.

Ximenia americana var. microphylla 102

Sour plum; suurpruim (Afrikaans); Sauerpflaume, Wilde Pflaume (German); omuninga (Herero)

The botanical name *Ximenia* commemorates a Spanish monk, Francisco Ximenez who wrote about the plants of Mexico in the 17th century. The genus belongs to the family Olacaceae whose distribution is given as evidence supporting land connections between continents in past geological ages.

Ximenia americana is widespread in tropical America, Asia and Africa. In America it is known as the American hog-plum. Variety *microphylla* meaning "small leaved" is found in southern Africa and in Namibia is limited to the northern half of the country. Another closely related plant, more common on the plateau, is *Ximenia caffra* (no. 103). It grows in the north-eastern parts of this country, the Transvaal, Botswana and northwards to tropical Africa.

Recent studies have shown that both these trees are hemi-parasites. In other words they form specialized roots capable of penetrating and absorbing food and other material from host plants. They can also penetrate inanimate objects like plastic, pebbles and charcoal.

The leaves of *Ximenia americana* are hairless, with a type of

removable waxy coating that makes the surface of the leaves whitish or bluish. This distinguishes them from *Ximenia caffra*.

The "ozoninga", as the fruits are called in Herero, supplement the diet of many indigenous people. These fruits are plum-like, about 3 cm long and fairly sour. The skin and stone are very bitter and are usually discarded. In Owambo a dye is made from mashed fruits and used for cloth or for palm leaves used in basketry. They are also made into beer in the Transvaal and elsewhere into various medicines.

Although the kernel of the pip is edible, it is more valued for its supply of oil. In the Kaokoveld the oil (sometimes pigmented red) may be used as a substitute for the fat which is rubbed into the body. While in Owambo the oil is used to soften leather. In some areas it is burnt as a torch.

The fruits of *Ximenia caffra* are more tasty and favoured when over-ripe. They make a good jelly rich in Vit C. The kernels have been investigated for their oil content, but although the quality of the oil would be suitable for commercial purposes, exploiting wild crops has not proved an economical proposition yet. In Owambo oil is expressed from the seed and mixed with red ochre as a cosmetic.

Although cultivated at the nursery in Grootfontein, both species are very slow growing and the long tap root makes transplanting difficult.

ALOE CIRCLE

Sansevieria pearsonii

Gemsbokhoring, kniesteker, (Afrikaans); Bajonettpflanze (German); ongwehe, ongwehe yozondundu (Herero)

There seems to be some confusion about which Italian prince the genus *Sansevieria* was named after, however there is no doubt about the validity of the common names. The rigid but fleshy leaves resemble "gemsbokhoring"
– (gemsbok horns) while the name "kniesteker" (knee pricker) has been earned from the spine-like tip of the leaf positioned at knee height. The species was named after Henry Pearson (1870-1916), a director of Kirstenbosch Botanic Gardens.

Sansevieria pearsonii forms dense colonies in certain relatively shady parts of the Waterberg. It also grows in the drier areas of the Transvaal, Natal, Swaziland, Zimbabwe and Botswana.

The leaves, which are grooved on one side, have a reddish-brown margin and grow from nodes on a creeping

rhizome. Stalks, about 50 cm long, bear tubular flowers that are almost hidden among the tough, fibrous leaves and surrounding grasses. The flowers are rather drab, varying in colour from cream to grey or olive green and usually occur in early spring. These result in more obvious and attractive orange berries.

In Owambo, threads are made by removing fibres from the leaves, pounding them between two pieces of wood and twisting them together. These threads are used in basket work and for making hats. Some fibres are made into heavier cord or rope by braiding or plaiting and used for harpoons or bow strings. Previously bundles of fibres, pounded until a fibrous mass, were dried and made into skirts for puberty rites of girls. *Sansevieria* plants can easily be propagated from rhizomes and they grow well in shady spots in the garden.

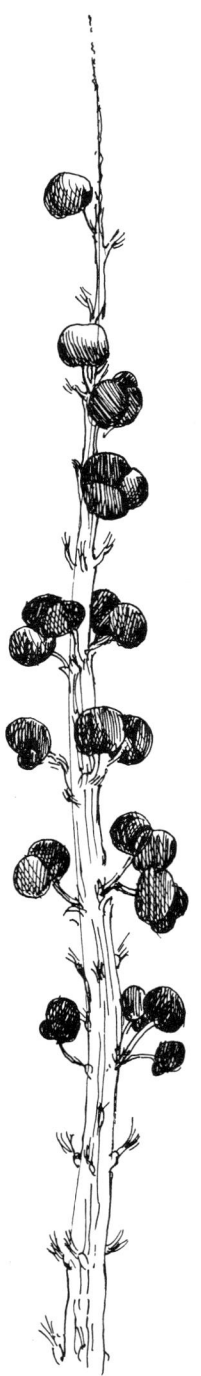

Aloe littoralis   29, 4

Windhoekaalwyn, bergaalwyn (Afrikaans); Bergaloe (German); otjindombo (Herero)

As the name "bergaalwyn" (mountain aloe) implies, this succulent is very common on hills throughout Namibia except in the far south. It seems strange therefore to learn that the botanical name – *littoralis* – means growing on the sea-shore and river banks. This is because it was first discovered and named by Welwitsch in 1854, growing in abundance, on the seaward side of the coastal hills just north of Luanda.

Aloe littoralis can also be found in Botswana, Zimbabwe, Mozambique and the Transvaal – where it is known as the mopane aloe. In Owambo a stemless form occurs that has spotted leaves. Usually only younger plants have spots.

Flowering time varies considerably over its distribution and is probably dependent on rain. If flowers occur in June in areas where *Aloe zebrina*, the "bontaalwyn", grows they are likely to hybridize.

Although the flowers of *Aloe littoralis* are rather flavourless, they are eaten straight from the plant, or collected "en masse" and cooked. Bushmen pound them into a soft, sticky substance and shape them into cakes. Apparently the nectar is a good source of sugar and the pollen is said to contain a rejuvenating property. The flowers provide vitamins and minerals.

During the dry years of the early 1970's a farmer in the vicinity of the Omatako Mountains noticed that baboons had eaten the lower ends of all the flower stalks. This section was sweet, unlike the bitter taste of most aloe leaves. This behaviour was not noticed in the following wetter years.

A study of an *Aloe littoralis* community in the Windhoek area highlighted a most interesting array of creatures that use them for shelter and foraging. The most obvious are scale insects, but others include spiders, plant-sucking bugs, various ants, weevils, flies and parasitoid wasps. At night moths also feed on the nectar and the dusky and scarlet chested sunbirds are among the most common birds to use this plant. Due to all this activity, potential seed production is reduced to about 20%.

Like all aloes of Namibia, it is protected, but seedlings are available from the nursery in Grootfontein. They grow very well, but need protection from frost when young and must not be over-watered.

Aloe littoralis is depicted on the Windhoek coat of arms.

Aloe zebrina

Bontaalwyn, sebra-aalwyn (Afrikaans); Zebra-Aloe (German); otjindombo, ondombo (Herero)

The only two aloes found at the Waterberg are known to hybridize with each other. *Aloe zebrina* is seldom seen along these paths, but it cannot be confused with any other Namibian aloe. It is the only spotted (Afrikaans – bont) one that grows in this country. The succulent leaves, about 30 cm long, grow in a rosette at ground level from where a metre long flower stalk grows, bearing reddish-orange flowers. The "bontaalwyn" can be found along the Mission Way, but may be missed among the undergrowth when not in flower.

Aloe zebrina grows in widely dispersed localities in southern Africa and varies considerably. As with *Aloe littoralis* the flowers are eaten and in Owambo they are also cooked, dried and stored for the dry season. At the Waterberg baboons utilize them, but the leaves are very bitter and never eaten.

Commiphora glandulosa 285, 1

Gewone kanniedood, (Afrikaans); omboo, omukange (Herero)

With their interesting peeling bark and spine-tipped shoots, these plants are easy to pick out along this route, in leaf or when leafless. They belong to the family that produces both frankincense and myrrh. The genus has over 200 species, of which at least 24 grow in Namibia and 12 are endemic. The word *Commiphora* means "to bear gum" and gum can sometimes be seen exuding from injured parts. The specific name *glandulosa* refers to glands on the calyx. *Commiphora* poles put into the ground strike readily, making living fences – hence the name "kanniedood" (never die).

In some publications *Commiphora glandulosa* falls under *Commiphora pyracanthoides*. The latter is then divided into two subspecies – *glandulosa* and *pyracanthoides*. However, although the distinction between the two subspecies is based on a number of small botanical details and a factor which is not applicable in this country – habit of growth – two seperate species are recognized today. It is interesting to note that the Bushmen have always recorded different uses for the two plants.

The distributions of *Commiphora glandulosa* and *C. pyracanthoides* overlap in Namibia and both occur in Botswana, the Transvaal, northern Cape and Zimbabwe. *Commiphora glandulosa* has rather inconspicuous flowers that

are green or reddish. Male flowers probably occur on different trees to the female flowers. The small fruit is reddish-green when young, but brown when ripe. It splits to show a black seed having a pseudaril with 4 bright red arms. This attracts birds especially hornbills.

The gum of *Commiphora glandulosa* is supposed to be edible, but that of *Commiphora pyracanthoides* is bitter and useless. In the Kaokoveld it is boiled in water to form a lather for washing clothes. A bark extract is used to straighten hair and it is also given to calves as a remedy for gallsickness. Wood of *Commiphora glandulosa* is made into cups or buckets, while in the Kaokoveld that of *C. pyracanthoides* is ground into a fine powder and used as tinder for flint lighters. Foliage may be heavily browsed and young shoots are eaten by duiker while elephant eat the bark.

The most valuable aspect of *Commiphora pyracanthoides* is the thirst-quenching property of the root. In times of need, roots are scraped and chewed. They are also eaten by wild animals from elephants to porcupines.

Commiphora pyracanthoides seedlings are available at the Grootfontein nursery and make attractive garden plants.

Grewia

An English physician and author of books on plants, Nehemiah Grew who lived between 1641 and 1712, has an interesting genus named after him – *Grewia*. It consists of over 400 species of shrubs or smallish trees that are widely distributed in Africa, Asia and Australia. About 26 occur in southern Africa.

Of the 7 species found at the Waterberg, none are particularly significant looking bushes and none are of any commercial value, but the fruits are an extremely important part of the eco-system. Interestingly enough, at first glance they appear to have too little flesh to be beneficial, but after a time, patience and chewing, their nutritional value becomes apparent. The berries are actually a good source of sugar and protein and as they can be stored, they have been the staple food of many indigenous people.

Grewia fruits are eaten raw or dried and may be soaked in water to make a drink or ground into meal. Many ripen in winter providing much needed fresh food in the dry months. Dried berries of *Grewia flava* are said to taste rather like sultanas, while others (e.g. *Grewia retinervis*) are first soaked and cooked. Some are stamped, made into meal and mixed with other foods e.g. locusts. In the Kaokoveld *Grewia flavescens* berries are soaked in water for a few days to make a refreshing 000023erage. Dried or fresh berries of different species are also fermented and distilled into brandy, like "olambika" in Owambo or "mampoer" of the Transvaal.

Although *Grewia* wood is considered to be of good quality, its uses are limited by the small size of most of the species. Nevertheless many articles are made e.g. arrow shafts, bows, walking sticks and knobkerries.

Grewia retinervis is used to make fire drill sockets and fish traps in Owambo, while frayed ends of small branches are used as tooth-brushes. The bark of the *Grewia flava* and *bicolor* were used as twine, while the former has been used to tune bows.

Grewias also have medicinal value and in the Kaokoveld *Grewia flavescens* is of religious significance, being utilized when approaching ancestral spirits. Flexible branches are also used in an oven for smoking garments. The Damara chew young parts of *Grewia flava* to treat cramps and stomachaches, while in Ovambo, roots were given to cattle as a remedy for pulmonary diseases. In Kaokoveld cows are dosed with a leaf extract to assist in expelling afterbirth. Poisoned arrow wounds were treated by spitting chewed leaves of *Grewia flavescens*, roots of *Grewia avellana* and *G. retinervis* onto them while inflammation caused by a large beetle were treated in the same way.

Leaves of most species are browsed by stock and game. In the Waterberg young stems and leaves of *Grewia retinervis* are eaten in summer, while *G. avellana* is utilized in winter, because its position under other trees protects it from frost.

Of the Grewias found at the Waterberg, only *Grewia flava* is limited to southern Africa. *Grewia bicolor, G. flavescens* and *G. villosa* even occur as far away as India, while the remainder grow in central and southern Africa with *Grewia tenax* reaching the Arabian Peninsular.

Except for the white flowers of *Grewia avellana* and *Grewia tenax*, the Waterberg grewias have yellow flowers. *Grewia flavescens* is probably the most abundant here and is noticeable because of its square stem, often seen climbing into other trees.

Seedlings of a few species are available at Grootfontein nursery for use as shrubs.

Grewia flava

Tree numbers and common names of the Waterberg Grewias:

Grewia avellana
Rosyntjiebos; Rosinenstrauch (German); omatakowavatwa (Herero)

Grewia bicolor 458
Rosyntjiebos (Afrikaans); Zweifarbiger Rosinenstrauch (German); omuvapu (Herero)

Grewia flava 459,1
Wild raisin; wilderosyntjie (Afrikaans); Gelbe Rosinenstrauch (German); omundjembere (Herero)

Grewia flavescens 459,2
Skurweblaarrosyntjiebos (Afrikaans); Gelbgrüner Rosinenstrauch (German); omuhe (Herero)

Grewia retinervia (=*deserticola*) 463,1
Kalahari grewia

Grewia tenax
Small-leafed white cross berry; kruisbessie (Afrikaans); Kreuzbeere (German); omundjendjere (Herero)

Grewia villosa 463,3
Malvarosyntjie, behaarde rosyntjie (Afrikaans); Zottiger Rosinenstrauch (German); omuhamati (Herero)

Mistletoe

Most normal plants manufacture their own food through photosynthesis and obtain water and dissolved mineral salts from the soil with their roots. There are however some plants, called parasites, that invade the tissues of other plants and extract food from these hosts. Their root sysems are usually highly specialized and the flowers and fruits are often large and brightly coloured to attract pollinators and birds to distribute seeds.

At the Waterberg, mistletoe of the Loranthaceae family are common and can be seen on diverse trees. They are actually hemiparasites i.e. they photosynthesize, but must obtain water and nutrients from a host plant. They are especially noticeable in winter when they flower.

In some cases the presence of a parasite may be advantageous to the host, however generaly the host suffers from the invasion and may eventually be killed off by the parasite. When the mistletoe dies off, evidence of its site of attachment to the host can easily be seen. These decorative growths on the host are called woodroses.

Tapinanthus oleifolius

Mistletoe; voëlent (Afrikaans); Streichholzpflanze (German); otjiraura (Herero)

In Owambo this mistletoe is known as "a-kind-of-leprosy" as it appears to cause "leprosy" on the marula tree. In Afrikaans it is called "voëlent" (bird graft or vaccination) as a seed will germinate on the stem of the host where it was wiped off or dropped by a bird.

At the Waterberg *Tapinanthus oleifolius* grows on a variety of hosts e.g. species of *Albizia, Acacia, Aloe, Combretum, Commiphora, Dichrostachys, Euclea, Ficus, Grewia, Rhus, Terminalia* and *Ziziphus.*

The generic name is derived form the Greek word *tapeinos* for "humble" and *anthos* "a flower", while *oleifolius* refers to its leaves which are said to resemble those of the olive. It is widespread throughout this country, much of Botswana and in the Transvaal and OFS.

Tapinanthus oleifolius is usually much-branched, greenish

and up to one metre tall, but its features, especially the leaves, vary considerably. The red flowers become berries that are red-orange when mature and they contain a sticky viscous substance inside. In Owambo this substance (called bird lime) is used to capture birds at water-holes. Tender branches are sometimes given to goats as feed and an infusion is taken for lumbago in Owambo.

Tapinanthus glaucocarpus

This species has a more limited distribution and number of hosts. It is parasitic on *Croton* species, but does occur on a few other plants as well. It is found only in northern and central Namibia and Angola.

Tapinanthus glaucocarpus is covered with dense, matted, woolly hairs, but becomes less hairy with maturity. The flowers are whitish-yellow from the long spreading hairs which cover it entirely. The ovoid berries are about 15 mm long.

Plicosepalus curviflorus

This mistletoe belongs to a genus found in the more arid regions of Africa. It is parasitic mainly on *Acacia* species, but may also be found on *Terminalia*. It occurs in the north-western Cape and Namibia. The berries are yellow and warty.

A similar species, found at the Waterberg, with flowers that are more pink and has red berries is *Plicosepalus kalachariensis*. It seems to be parasitic only on *Acacia* species and is widespread in northern Namibia, Botswana, the Transvaal, Swaziland and Natal.

Ferns

Ten ferns have been collected in the Waterberg Plateau Park, with only one (*Cheilanthes dinteri*) endemic to Namibia and Angola. The others are found throughout the world or are limited to the African continent. Although some are widespread, in Namibia they may be confined to the Waterberg region.

Microlepia speluncae

The only fern in the Waterberg known to be edible is *Ophioglossum polyphyllum* [adder's tongue fern; Natternzunge (German); omundove (Herero)]. It occurs from Arabia to southern Africa and is used in various parts as wild spinach.

A few have medicinal value: a decoction of the rhizome of *Pellaea calomelanos* has been used for boils and pimples in the nose and mouth. It is also given to children as a tranquiliser after being crushed in milk and a decoction may be used with other plants as an anthelmintic. A decoction of the rhizome of *Ceterach cordatum* is used for colds and sore throats.

A warm decoction of the green parts of the adder's tongue are used as a lotion for boils, while the bittersweet and slightly astringent foliage of *Adiantum capillus-veneris* [Venus, Frauenhaarfarn (German)] is used for chest complaints. Dried and powdered leafy parts of *Ceterach cordatum* were formerly used in southern Europe for diseases of the spleen, while smoked leaves of *Pelleae calomelanos* may be used by Africans for treating asthma.

A fern that is frequently seen along the Kambazembi Walking Route is *Pellaea calomelanus,* also known as the "hard fern". The word *pellos* means dark or dusty and refers to its dark axis (or stem), while the species name comes from *calo* (beautiful) and *melanos* (black). It is found throughout southern and tropical Africa as well as in places like Spain and India. It is well adapted to exposed conditions, having leathery leaves, which are however unusual in that they do not have any protective hairs.

Cheilanthes marlothii unlike the above species is very hairy. It responds very quickly to rainfall, but generally looks dry in the rock crevices and around boulders where it grows. It is limited to Angola, Namibia and the Transvaal. Like *Cheilanthes dinteri* it can usually be found on the southern aspects of slopes.

Microlepia speluncae although occurring throughout central and southern Africa has so far only been recorded from the Waterberg in Namibia. It is confined to moist shaded places and varies considerably. It flourishes at the fountain on the Forest Walk, where the fronds can be a metre long or more. No uses have been recorded for it.

Cheilanthes marlothii

Pellaea calomelanos

Lichens (Contributed by Dr. D. Wessels)

A lichen consists of two partners, the mycobiont (which is a fungus) and a photobiont which can be a green algae or a blue-green bacterium. The dominant partner is the fungus, thus lichens are classified as fungi, which include the mushrooms, bread moulds and sac fungi. Lichens do not form stems, leaves or roots like higher plants and the structure we see is known as a thallus. Although lichens are not particularly conspicuous in nature, they are very important. They take part in natural metabolic processes i.e. oxygen and carbon dioxide cycles, contribute to the formation of soil and colonize new habitats.

The partners of the lichen live together symbiotically. During the day the photobiont converts carbon dioxide from air and water present in the thallus into sugars i.e. it photosynthesises. The mycobiont uses these sugars and in return provides water and elements as well as protection to the photobiont. Dissolved nutrients are taken up by the whole surface of the thallus. Reproduction in lichens can be by means of fragments, distinctive vegetative reproductive structures or by spores.

Lichens are extremely hardy organisms that occur in virtually every environment – from ice deserts, dry desert plains to tropical woods. They survive severe environmental conditions in a metabolically inactive state. This characteristic in part explains their extremely slow growth and some of the lichens actively growing in the Waterberg Park today, were probably already decades old when the rocks were engraved by earlier inhabitants of the area. Lichens were possibly the first group of organisms to colonize the bare sandstone.

Although the lichen flora of the Waterberg Pleateau Park has not been intensively studied, an estimated 140 species occur in the park. There is a rich variety growing on rock and bark and some species are unique to the Waterberg and do not occur anywhere else in the world. Some lichens even occur in the seasonal rock pools and drainage canals of the sandstone.

When the photobiont is a bluegreen bacterium, the species is known as a cyanophyllic lichen. They play an important part in the primary colonization of bare areas. Millions of cyanophyllic lichens, green algae and bluegreen bacteria, although not individually visible to the naked eye, form the black strips that are so characteristic of the sandstone ridges that surround the plateau.

By far the largest group of lichens in the Waterberg Plateau Park have green algae as the photobiont. Lichenologists divide this group, for convenience, according to their growth form into foliose [leafy] and fruticose [shrubby] types. The thalli of the latter are upright or pendulous and branched and grow on tree stumps and rocks. Many different species occur in this park.

Insects use lichens as a source of food, protection and even camouflage. In the Waterberg the foliose types provide different mite species with food and shelter, while moth larvae eat both the foliose and fructose lichens. Sometimes one may be fortunate enough to find a bagworm that uses lichens as a source of food and building material.

Crustose lichens form a thin, flat crust that is strongly attached to the surface on which they grow. Numerous species occur on the Waterberg sandstone and these lichens are responsible for the spectacular colour mosaics on the otherwise red rocks. Distinctive substances produced by the symbiont (lichen acids) give rise to the colour of the thalli. In bygone days these substances were used to colour the purple garments of kings.

Another group of lichens, namely endolithic lichens, form a very important part of the lichen flora of the Waterberg Park. Due to chemical and mechanical wheathering, they can bury themselves into the sandstone. The light flecks or spots in the red sandstone that can be seen with the naked eye are actually the thalli of these lichens. Endolithic lichens actively tunnel into the sandstone. As the lichen grows deeper into the sandstone, dislodged quartz grains on top of the thallus eventually fall on to the soil surface. Thus endolithic lichens, together with natural weathering processes have given rise to the striking figures and mushroom shapes of the rocks on top of the plateau at the Waterberg Plateau Park.

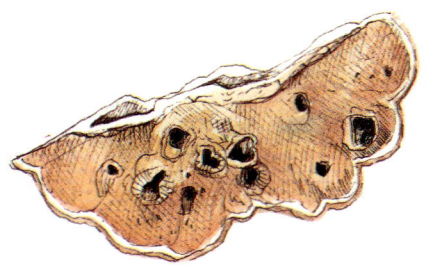

Trametes cingulata

Journals and magazines consulted:

Bothalia
Botswana Notes and News
Custos
Dendron
Dinteria
Flora of Southern Africa
Landbouweekblad
On Record
Prodromus einer Flora von Südwestafrika
Roan News
Scientiae
Scientific Society of SWA/N

Books:

Berry, C., (no date). *Trees and Shrubs of the Etosha National Park*. Multi Services, Windhoek.
Carr, J. D., 1976. *The South African Acacias*. Conservation Press, Johannesburg.
Carr, J. D., 1988. *Combretaceae in Southern Africa*. Tree Society of Southern Africa.
Directorate of Forestry, Pamphlet on 317, 1984. *The Wild Fig, tree of the year*.
Jankowitz, W. J., 1983. *Die Plantekologie van die Waterberg Platopark*. Unpublished manuscript of Doctoral thesis.
Le Roux, P. J., 1971. *The common names and a few uses of the better known indigenous plants of South West Africa*, Dept. Forest. Bull. 47.
Malan, J. S. and Owen Smith, G. L., 1974. *The Ethnobotany of Kaokoland*. Cimbebasia Ser. B, vol. 2 no 5.
Palmer, E. and Pitman N., 1973. *Trees of Southern Africa*. 3 vols. Balkema, Cape Town.
Rodin, R. J., 1985. *The Ethnobotany of the Kwanyama Ovambos*. Monographs in Systematic Botany from the Missouri Botanical Garden vol. 9.
Von Breitenbach, F., 1986. *National List of Indigenous Trees*. Dendrological Foundation.
Von Koenen, E., 1977. *Heil- und Giftpflanzen in Südwestafrika*. Akademisher Verlag Windhoek, SWA.
Visser, J., 1981. *South African Parasitic Flowering Plants*. Juta, Cape Town.

Index

	Tree No.	Page
Acacia ataxacantha	160	31
A. erioloba	168	17
A. erubescens	164	25
A. fleckii	165	25
A. hebeclada subsp. *hebeclada*	170	33
A. hereroensis	171	68
A. karroo	172	20
A. luederitzii var. *luederitzii*	174	43
A. mellifera subsp. *detinens*	176	28
A. mellifera subsp. *mellifera*	176, 1	28
A. reficiens subsp. *reficiens*	181	43
A. tortilis subsp. *heteracantha*	188	41
A. tortilis subsp. *spirocarpa*	188, 1	41
Adiantum capillus-veneris		130
Albizia anthelmintica	150	21
Aloe littoralis	29, 4	117
A. zebrina		118
Boscia albitrunca	122	11
Ceterach cordatum		130
Cheilanthes dinteri		129
C. marlothii		130
Combretum apiculatum subsp. *apiculatum*	532	49
Combretum apiculatum subsp. *leutweinii*	532, 1	49
C. collinum	541	52
C. hereroense	538	52
C. imberbe	539	105
C. molle	537	52
C. psidioides subsp. *dinteri*	543, 1	52
C. zeyheri	546	52
Commiphora angolensis	272	66
C. glandulosa	285, 1	119
C. pyracanthoides	285	119
C. tenuipetiolata	289	66
Croton gratissimus	328	58
Dichrostachys cinerea subsp. *africana*	190	101
Dombeya rotundifolia	471	71
Drosera burkeana		8
Erythrina decora	243	84
Euclea undulata var. *myrtina*	601, 1	107
Ferns		129

Ficus cordata	51	53
F. ilicina (= F. geurichiana)	53	77
F. sycomorus	66	90
Fungus		136
Grewia avellana		124
G. bicolor	458	123
G. flava	459, 1	123
G. flavescens	459, 2	123
G. retinervis (= G. deserticola)	463, 1	123
G. tenax		124
G. villosa	463, 3	124
Kirkia acuminata	267	79
Lichens		132
Lonchocarpus nelsii	239	63
Maerua juncea		37
M. schinzii	136	34
Microlepia speluncae		130
Obetia carruthersiana	69	57
Ophioglossum polyphyllum		130
Osyris lanceolata	100	73
Pellaea calomelanos		130
Peltophorum africanum	215	46
Plicosepalus curviflorus		128
P. kalachariensis		128
Rhus ciliata		96
Rhus lancea	386	93
R. marlothii	389, 2	96
R. tenuinervis	393, 2	96
Sanserveria pearsonii		113
Securinega virosa	309	61
Steganotaenia araliacea	569	81
Tapinanthus glaucocarpus		128
T. oleifolius		127
Terminalia brachystemma	548	16
T. prunioides	550	13
T sericea	551	16
Trametes cingulata		136
Ximenia americana var. *microphylla*	102	111
X. caffra	103	111
Ziziphus mucronata	447	97

Index

Tree No.		Page
29,4	*Aloe littoralis*	117
51	*Ficus cordata*	53
53	*F. ilicina* (= *F. guerichiana*)	77
66	*F. sycomorus*	90
69	*Obetia carruthersiana*	57
100	*Osyris lanceolata*	73
102	*Ximenia americana* var. *microphylla*	111
103	*X. caffra*	111
122	*Boscia albitrunca*	11
136	*Maerua schinzii*	34
150	*Albizia anthelmintica*	21
160	*Acacia ataxacantha*	31
168	*A. erioloba*	17
164	*A. erubescens*	25
165	*A. fleckii*	25
170	*A. hebeclada* subsp. *hebeclada*	33
171	*A. hereroensis*	68
172	*A. karroo*	20
174	*A. luederitzii* var. *luederitzii*	43
176	*A. mellifera* subsp. *detinens*	28
181	*A. reficiens* subsp. *reficiens*	43
188	*A. tortilis* subsp. *heteracantha*	41
188,1	*A. tortilis* subsp. *spirocarpa*	41
190	*Dichrostachys cinerea* subsp. *africana*	101
215	*Peltophorum africanum*	46
239	*Lonchocarpus nelsii*	63
243	*Erythrina decora*	84
267	*Kirkia acuminata*	79
272	*Commiphora angolensis*	66
285	*C. pyracanthoides*	119
285,1	*C. glandulosa*	119
289	*C. tenuipetiolata*	66
309	*Securinega virosa*	61
328	*Croton gratissimus*	58
386	*Rhus lancea*	93
389,2	*R. marlothii*	96
393,2	*R. tenuinervis*	96
447	*Ziziphus mucronata*	97
458	*Grewia bicolor*	123
459,1	*G. flava*	123

459,2	G. flavescens	123
463,1	G. retinervis (= G. deserticola)	123
463,3	G. villosa	124
471	Dombeya rotundifolia	71
532	Combretum apiculatum subsp. apiculatum	49
532,1	Combretum apiculatum subsp. leutweinii..	49
537	C. molle	52
538	C. hereroense	52
539	C. imberbe	105
541	C. collinum	52
543,1	C. psidioides subsp. dinteri	52
546	C. zeyheri	52
548	Terminalia brachystemma	16
550	T. prunioides	13
551	T. sericea	16
569	Steganotaenia araliacea	81
601,1	Euclea undulata var. myrtina	107

NOTES

NOTES

© Gamsberg Publishers,
P.O. Box 22830,
Windhoek, 9000

Printed and bound by
National Book Printers
Goodwood, Cape
ISBN 0-86848-589-6